So you really want to buy a pub?

. . . .

Steve Broadbent

So you really want to buy a pub?

. . . .

Steve Broadbent

Airworthy Publications
International Limited

FIRST PUBLISHED IN 1999 IN GREAT BRITAIN
BY AIRWORTHY PUBLICATIONS INTERNATIONAL LIMITED,
BASSFIELD SOUTH, MANCHESTER ROAD
WALMERSLEY, BURY,
LANCASHIRE BL9 5LY

COPYRIGHT © AIRWORTHY PUBLICATIONS INTERNATIONAL LIMITED

ISBN 0952 8845-3-4

WRITTEN BY STEVE BROADBENT
DESIGNED BY VIV HARPER

DEDICATION

I have always wanted to write a book, and books need dedications to remember those who have influenced the writer. This book could well be, and indeed is, dedicated to my wife, Viv, and my father and her's. But I have spent most of my career in and around aeroplanes of one sort or another and they have given me many experiences I shall, God Willing, mull over time and time again as I grow older.

So this book is really dedicated to eight friends and former colleagues who will not be able to share that pleasure, eight who have been so tragically killed in flying accidents around the world and over the years, and especially to

Brian Edward Helm

killed over Zagreb in 1976, for whom the first pint in our pub would have been pulled.

And also to my aunt Joan, who died in 1998 and who was kind enough to remember me in her Will with a generous bequest that enabled this book to be published.

. . . .

Acknowledgements

With thanks to The Good Guys…

Richard and Wilfred the Solicitors, and Peter the Accountant

Doug and Tony the Bank Managers, and others at the Bank

And our Trainer, who must remain anonymous for fear of identifying the Bad Guys.

Without the solid advice from the Good Guys, the Bad Guys would have had us move into a pub, a life and a set of values for which we were not suited or prepared.

And special thanks to Kay Print Service, Bradford (01274 865818), who supplied the super cartoons which enliven the boring text!

Playbill

. . . .

Introduction and Prelude to Act One
The gender thing – let's get the sex out of the way first!   *1*

ACT ONE: Getting the basics right   7

Scene One: It takes two – how is your relationship?   7
Scene Two: But what sort of person are you –
    will you make the grade as a landlord??   *10*
Scene Three: The commitment   *12*
Scene Four: Staff, honesty and holidays   *15*

ACT TWO: What is the right pub for you –
    location, location, location   *19*

Scene One: Location, type and brewery ties   *20*
Scene Two: Get the best advice   *49*
Scene Three: Starting the search   *61*
Scene Four: Analysing promising pubs   *70*

Intermission: Pubs and money, or lack of it   77

ACT THREE: Towards changeover day, carefully   *91*

Scene One: Training and learning   *91*
Scene Two: Getting there, making a bid and moving forward   *98*
Scene Three: Entering the final lap   *106*

The curtain falls: Changeover day   *111*

Strike the set: Our diary   *119*

. . . .

Introduction and Prelude to Act One

SETTING THE SCENE

From the American comedy TV show *Cheers*. Cheers is a Boston bar once owned by Sam Malone: Sam had to sell it to Rebecca, who is now dating Robin Colcord, a British millionaire. Sam now works for Rebecca in Cheers, but wants his own bar again: he is discussing his plan to buy a closed bar in a seedy part of Boston's docks with Robin.

Robin: "So what you are finally saying is that you are going to re-open the same business in the same location where it went belly-up just last year?"

Sam: "No, no, you see this is going to be new, this is very different – now it's Sam's Place."

Robin: "What was it before?"

Sam: "Tim's Place."

Robin: "This could work.... by work, I mean if you pour every dime into the place, struggle, scrimp and save and somehow hang on during the lean years, hope there is no recession, you might just begin to

. . . .

show a profit. After that, well, you might scrape a living, a dismal living...."

Sam "OK, so what's the downside?"

Viv and I went down the same path and very nearly didn't heed the various Robins in our lives.... If you are going to buy a pub, or indeed any business, listen to all opinions, especially the ones you don't want to hear.

PRELUDE TO ACT ONE

By the time you have got as far as reading these words, perhaps browsing in a book shop or at your local library, you will doubtless have given a lot of thought to that long-held dream of running your own public house.

Whether it is because of changing employment patterns and younger people can no longer settle in to life-long "blue collar" jobs as industries come and go, or whether it is because more and more "white collar" people are taking early retirement or are being made redundant in their 50s, or whether it is because people are seeing the life of a publican as being far preferable to the daily rat race and the incessant commuting for hours in crowded trains or choked motorways – for whatever reason, more and more people are wanting to run their own pubs. At the same time, more and more companies are either setting up as operators of pub chains, or are expanding their chains, and this gives "the man in the street" the impression that it is a booming industry, offering safe and lucrative employment.

You may well have read through other books, for, since there are a growing number of people seeking to become landlords, there are also more people keen to advise them. Conventional wisdom tells us that there is greater wealth in advising than doing. One thing about this book is immediately apparent: it contains absolutely no advertisements of, or endorsements for, pub-related products and services. In preparing this book we (meaning me and my wife, Viv) have wanted to keep it as we ourselves would have liked to have been in our dream pub – totally independent, behoven to no-one for our well-being. I cannot, of course, say bad things about named people or companies, but at least by not having advertising we can avoid having to say nice things we might not altogether agree with.

This book also contains, or rather does not contain, one ingredient vital to any book of advice – experience in running a pub – and you might think that this precludes this book being of value on your search. But in that search you need every bit of advice you can get, so you need this book and others, for starters. We tried for nine long and hard months to buy a pub – five entirely different ones in fact – and then gave up. The system beat us, and we feel others should benefit from our lack of actual hands-on experience: better to abandon plans before they turn to disaster than afterwards, or at least better to set sail knowing for sure whether the earth is flat or round.

So, this book is all about how to buy a pub, or in our case not buy a pub, and the pitfalls we encountered. It is not about running a pub, licensing law, food hygiene and a number of other things which you will find out about on your way towards buying a pub and which are well covered either in other books, or better from your point of view, in the training courses you will need to go on.

The text divides into three Acts. Act One is about the type of people you will need to be and the commitment you will have to make. Act Two tells you about the types of pub and starts you thinking as to where you might want to live: it also discusses the people you will meet on the journey and the actions you need to take once you have firmly committed to looking for that ideal place. An intermission looks at the profitability of pubs, and how little there might be: Act Three examines your moves as you make a bid for a pub, have it accepted and head towards pulling your first pint.

Finally, as you enjoy an after-theatre drink and the set is being struck, comes our very personal diary of those nine months of endeavour, with all the names changed to protect the guilty, so you can see that it is not all plain sailing.

Good Luck in your search: we are sure running a pub can be both idyllic rewarding, and doubtless it suits many people. But, as our first piece of advice, before going beyond this book and the others you will buy, give that dream even more thought.

(And finally, to lay down our qualifications for passing such comments, this book is being largely written by Steve, 51 years young as of this day. Viv and I have been married ten years and have no children, but have seen in our researches time and time again how pubs and kids don't mix. And, as you will see later, we very nearly ran a pub – Viv was for six months the licensee of a pub which never opened, and Steve was more than happy to see her name over the door and concentrate his efforts as part of an equal opportunity closely-knit team.)

The gender thing – let's get the sex out of the way first

In this humble book, simply to save space and linguistic complexity, the sexist nouns such as landlord and barmaid are used indiscriminately, and are to be taken by you, dear reader, as including both sexes: landlady and barman, waiter, bar tender are all equally valid words. Similarly the male pronoun is used, that is he/him and his, when the female and plural equivalents are just as applicable. I also use 'man' and 'woman' to denote individuals of male and female genders. No implications with regard to age or social class are intended by the absence of such words as lady or girl, lad or bloke. and, to set the minds of the sensitive at ease, when, as you will read in the final section *(Strike the Set)*, we applied and were granted a licence for a pub, it was in the name of my wife alone, for it suited us better that way. Her name was above the door, or actually it wasn't as we never got as far as having the board made up!!

One day someone will invent a non-gender specific pronoun, but for this writer politically correct words such as landperson are plain daft. If this attitude annoys you we apologise, but if you get annoyed by such trivial irritations, be aware there are some pretty big dinosaurs out there to really get under your skin!!

But there is a serious point. There is one type of person, besides the criminal fraternity and the certifiably insane (and some would say that most landlords fall into at least one, if not both of those categories!), who cannot run a pub – single people. However dynamic and erudite you are, it takes two, at least, and two in close harmony at that. There is nothing in a pub that a man can do that a woman can not, and the roles and duties of the landlord and his partner are entirely interchangeable on an almost minute by minute basis, as are all the other tasks involved in running your own pub business – marketing manager, financial director, head of purchasing, chief washer-up, plumber's mate, electrician's bag-holder and senior vice president in charge of mopping up sick are all non-gender specific, and whoever is doing one one minute, may well be doing another the next as well as drawing pints of foaming ale and smiling sweetly.

Above all this is a personal story, with the lessons we learnt and the experiences we went through. It does not, however, pretend to be comprehensive or authoratative: following the words in this book by no means guarentees success, but they might give you one or two pointers as to how to avoid failure, heartache and misery – but even that is by no means assured!

Steve Broadbent
Bury, May-December 1998

Act 1

GETTING THE BASICS RIGHT

The scene is set largely in a lounge, and also in the bedroom, of a family home somewhere in Great Britain. Time: the present.

SCENE ONE:

IT TAKES TWO – HOW IS YOUR RELATIONSHIP?

But it does take two. You may well be man and wife, woman and husband, or partners, and if you are, you need to have a well-established and very stable relationship. If one of you likes to chat all the time, giving lip-service to the task in hand while your partner chases round like a headless chicken, you will get nowhere. If you feel washing up is a woman's job, ditto, and if you are the kind who gets insanely and irrationally jealous if your man even gives you a paranoid suspicion that he is looking in the direction of another woman, then how are you going to cope with the arrival of female customers (of which there are a growing number in pubs – indeed it is the biggest growth sector), let alone a barmaid having, shall we say, the more traditional physical virtues. You need to be two people working as one, filling in when the other is busy, always looking to offer support. Think hard. If that is not you and your partner, perhaps it is already time to find another book to read. Jack and Vera Duckworth of *The Rover's Return, Coronation Street*, are not ideal role models!

Of course, you don't have to be a married heterosexual couple. In these enlightened times, who is going to bat an eyelid if the two "bosses" are unmarried, or of the same gender. But, unless you are a gay couple running a gay bar in a gay area, do be careful not to offend those less liberal minded. As I shall say time and time again in these pages, the profit margins in the industry are woefully thin, and one customer offended is one customer who will not come back, and perhaps as many as ten who will hear the bad impression gained and not even think of visiting. You need every customer you can get across the threshold and more, so keep not only domestic arguments and lovers' tiffs in the owners' accommodation (if you have to have them at all – if you are arguing you are not running a smooth and efficient ship) but any personal predilections, of whatever nature, well away from anyone who might be even slightly offended.

Of course, many other types of partnership are very valid for running a pub – father and daughter (age and wisdom coupled with youthful energy), siblings, ordinary business partners not involved emotionally, better still, a whole family unit of parents and adult children, and even their spouses!

HANDY TIP ONE

A customer who leaves with a grievance which he or she perceives to be the fault of someone or something in your pub will tell, on average, ten other people, all potential customers, of your shortfall. A customer who leaves happy may well recommend your establishment to his or her friends. You cannot afford to have grievances, however ill-founded, leaving your pub. Customer service is all, the customer is king!

Another thing you might not want to be, in addition to being landlord and all the other jobs noted above, is the parent of a young child. Pubs are no place for children at all in our contentious opinion, but they are certainly no place for the young children of the landlord to grow up in or, heaven forbid, run about in as if the public area was their private play area. The domestic accommodation of most pubs is very small and there is often hardly the space "upstairs" for children to play with their friends, or to study in peace when they start having homework and exams, so you will need to give this aspect careful thought. Just where in your chosen pub can Little Johnnie live, study and play without upsetting customers, getting secret access to alcohol, being damaged by cigarette smoke and colourful language, or getting under parents' feet while they are trying to do the accounts? If there

But, unless you are a gay couple running a gay bar in a gay area, do be careful not to offend those less liberal minded.

is not space, facilities and necessary privacy for all of your family, then, again, are pubs for you?

And, again, it really does take two to run the pub. If you and your partner have young children, or have decided to have them once the business is underway, then that means that not only is one parent going to be out of commission during the birth, but one person is also going to be 100% occupied with parental duties, at least until the child goes to school. Heaven help you if you have a second and third.... If one parent is parenting they are not looking after the business, and the other parent, by definition, has neither the time to run the pub properly, nor to enjoy all the undoubted benefits of midnight feeds and nappy changing....

The Catch 22 is that pubs need energy. The sort of energy you have in your 20s and 30s when you may well have or want to have children, not the sort of lack of energy that comes with being 50 or 60, the time when the children have left home and you want to take up that dream of running your own pub.

And another job? We once viewed a pub where the wife ran the operation "to give her something to do" while the man carried on his macho-style "full-time" job. The result I will leave to your imagination.

So, to run a pub properly you need to be in a permanent relationship which is as free from stress and argument as possible, with maximum mutual support being the order of the day. You really ought to have the kids, if any, grown up and left home, yet you also both need the energy of the young, coupled with the wisdom of age. Above all, you need to be non-gender specific in your outlook – a job is a job, and the job of running a pub has a very big capital J!!

Scene Two

BUT WHAT SORT OF PERSON ARE YOU? WILL YOU MAKE A GOOD LANDLORD?

If you have not already done so, visit a pub.

Well, joking apart, I am sure you have done so many times, but perhaps you have your own favourite local where you go at specific times, maybe weekly for a meal, maybe every night for a swift half on your way home from work or before closing time, maybe just at lunchtimes. Probably your desire to run your own pub has been nurtured by seeing your "hosts" seemingly having a lovely time chatting and drinking and generally socialising with all and sundry every day of the week – what a wonderful life! Of course, what you cannot see is the furious way they are paddling to keep their heads above water, out of sight of the public. You need to visit pubs, plural, with a critical eye, four critical eyes if possible!

Before you can even think of buying a pub, you need to make sure you will like the life, at least the bits you can see. Start going to other pubs in the district, even if they are not the type you might want to run, and at different times. If they are "not usually the thing for you" go to a karaoke night, and then remember your pub may well have to have one "by popular demand" every week. That's every week.

Similarly, choose times when the pub is going to be quiet. Sit there with your halves of shandy, alone, and think how you would feel as landlord with all the lights blazing, food prepared but unsold, the central heating boiler on full – and there are only two strangers in the whole place. How can you pay the bills? We once "mystery visited" a pub we were interested in at 1.15 on a weekday lunchtime – there was no-one else in and mine was the first pint pulled that day. Could we have stood the solitude? Then another pub we got very interested in had 72 people in at a spot count on a Friday lunchtime, all high-spenders – and over 40 on a wet January Monday at noon. Could we have stood the pace? (More on mystery visiting later: the intriguing point of these two pubs was that they had very similar declared annual takings.)

So, without spending a penny extra, well, not many, make a broad assessment of the task you are heading for, one based on many pubs at different times, rather than the seeming bed of roses which surrounds your usual local. Get used to assessing every pub you go in – is there a friendly welcome, is the beer good, what are the prices like, is the food hot, good value and well-presented, are the notices easy to read and appealing, etc., etc? These and one thousand and one other things you will need to be able to judge as you get more and more seriously interested and lead towards that Purchasing Decision.

And start learning on Day One and applying what you learn to your future pub. Every time you go into a pub look closely at what they offer and how they do it, and what features you want to copy, modify or avoid in yours – bar staff in uniforms, menus creatively designed, scribbled and hidden chalkboards, real flowers in the Ladies, a big screen TV, an eye-catching display of whiskies... what would you like in your pub? Make notes of the "wants" and the "avoids" for future reference.

And what kind of people are you? There are tall landlords and short ones, fat and thin, smiling and grumpy, welcoming and off-hand, and, doubtless, those who are less honest than others, less diligent, less law-abiding or less industrious. It takes all sorts as in any walk of life. But what sort of person are you? Pub running is VERY competitive, and you, as newcomers with an urge to make a pound or two, have to be the welcoming, friendly and avuncular sort.

SCENE THREE

THE COMMITMENT

Most books I have read say being a landlord is a 70 hours a week job. It is not. It is all too apparent that it is much, much more!!

So far I have asked you to assess pubs in general to see if you really feel they are for you, and by visiting different pubs at different times you will be getting a feel for the type of pub you might like to operate, in what sort of area and what part of the country, and I will return to these aspects later.

But, if you still feel you can cope with the hurly-burly of a karaoke night and the loneliness of a snowy February lunchtime when no one arrives at all, let's now look at the lifestyle you will be enjoying.

Now the law says that the licensee shall be on the premises at all times the pub is open, but this, like so many aspects of licensing law, is neither practical nor common sense. However, if you do leave the premises, whether to go to the bank, the cash-and-carry, the mother-in-law's or the Algarve, and the person you leave in charge allows drugs to be sold in the bar and drinks to be bought till 1am, then it is you who will be prosecuted and your licence that may well be forfeited. And, just to add salt to the wound, if you lose your licence and you are a tenant, you will still be paying the rent until you can sell the business to another. Such aspects might make you think that, at least until you are firmly in command with all systems running smoothly, you will not only want to be behind the bar at all times, but that you will want to be there for your own peace of mind.

Today, most pubs are open from before noon till close to midnight, seven days a week, 365 days a year. I know it is obvious, but pubs, unlike all other privately-run retail outlets, don't have half day closing. And Bank Holidays, when most folk are away enjoying other people's pubs, are your busiest days, hopefully!!

So at least for the first few months until you can really trust others, you are going to be behind the bar for around 12 hours a day. Meals will be taken at quiet times, probably "on the hoof", and, by the by, you are going to need a pretty strong constitution not to be tempted by such prolonged and close proximity to all manner of alcoholic

Most books I have read say being a landlord is a 70 hours a week job. It is not. It is all too apparent that it is much, much more!!

beverages – drinking on duty is not only a slippery slope, it also kills the very small profit margins you will be working with.

But there is far more to do than just stand behind the bar, greeting each customer with cheerfulness and bonhomie. Clearly, all throughout your opening hours you will be keeping shelves stocked, tables clean and cleared, a regular check on the toilets is a good idea, and barrels will need changing over from time to time. And, while you will want to encourage them to call outside of opening hours, there will be a steady stream of would-be-suppliers' sales representatives calling to try and sell their wares, calls that may well be ever more frequent if you get in the habit of offering them a beer on the house while they are with you – saves them buying their own lunch! A quick word on reps. While doing our preliminary research a rep called at a pub where I was one of very few customers, eating my lunch. The rep held a long and detailed conversation at the next table about his product range – essential items for ladies toilets – which rather put me off my food! Do be discreet with reps, and don't encourage the ones you don't need.

In the morning, before opening time, there will be all sorts to do – supervise the cleaning, cleaning out the beer lines at least once a week, making up orders for drinks and food suppliers, preparing menus, liaising with the chef, taking umpteen telephone calls from staff who are sick, students wanting jobs, people wanting to make appointments to see you or take orders for goods or bookings for tables....

Then there's the accounts to keep – again more later on this task – and cash to take to the bank at least twice a week, better more often. Make sure you have enough change, that the staff rotas are prepared, that staff hours are logged and wage packets are made up promptly, and, literally, 1001 other things.

And oh, you have to eat. If you don't you will die. Irregular and hasty meals make for the rapid onset of ill-health, so you will need to have a routine of eating properly, but not when you are serving. You may want to arrange alternating times with your partner, so you each get breaks during the day, but don't forget, while you are resting, the other person is doing twice as much, their share and yours!

And after closing time, have you ever noticed how folk don't seem to have homes to go to? No matter what the law says about last orders and drinking up time, (assuming you "close" at 11.00pm) you can bet on busy nights it will be 11.30 at least before you can lock the doors and do your closing security check, during which you find some drunkard has trashed the toilets! And if you are anything like me, with all that buzzing round your head and all the thoughts of the next day's tasks, you might find it hard to get to sleep.

All in all then, at least until you can really really trust the staff, it is at least 15 hours a day, 100+ hours a week, 5000+ hours a year Commitment

——————— Pause for thought ———————

SCENE FOUR

STAFF, HONESTY AND HOLIDAYS

While this is primarily a book to take you through the decision-making process from glint-in-the-eye to changeover day, and therefore staff are not really its concern, as I have mentioned them in the previous paragraphs, a word about "the team" might be in order here.

If, as will almost certainly be the case, you are taking over a fully-operational pub, you will also be taking over a fully-operational team of bar staff – indeed an early task once you have agreed a purchase is to get all the staff and the out-going owner together, first to break the news of the departure of their beloved leader and then to introduce yourself and assure everyone that, no matter what your plans are in reality, all their jobs are safe and that truly and honestly, while you are sure Jack the Landlord is a most splendid fellow, you and your partner have every wish to be as good and at least as successful! If your reassurances don't work or the staff take a dislike to you, then they may well leave along with their landlord, and you will have the huge and unwanted headache of finding replacements just at the time you have far better things to think about. In your first weeks you will need good, reliable, well-trained and experienced staff who can cover up for your newness and in whose hands the continuing excellence of the business is safe.

The trouble is, most staff will be clever enough to realise your weaknesses, and, while outgoing Jack might have had the measure of them, there are a whole raft of tricks they might get up to if you don't have eyes in the back of your head until mutual respect is earned and established. Sadly, as in all walks of life, some bar staff will be less than 100% honest, and if they only go as far as pouring themselves and a few friends a free drink while you are taking your evening snack you will be lucky. Honest and dependable staff are worth far more than the miserable wage you are likely to want to pay them, so treat the best properly and you will have a good foundation.

Again, something that will be discussed later on is the need to keep a close eye on gross profit percentage, the figure all pubs seem to be ruled by. If you carry out a regular, by which I mean at least monthly, check on stock, this figure will give you a very good idea if someone is pushing their luck. Don't forget, margins are so small that any illicit activity, however harmless the perpetrator thinks it is, ("I have worked very hard all day, Jack always let us have a Scotch before going home." More fool Jack!!), will eat deeply into your bottom line when totalled up over 365 days.

In talking with other publicans you will hear of their frequent holidays, often abroad. That may lead you to believe that it is an easy and profitable existence, and the idea of two or three holidays in Tenerife or the Algarve may seem far better than your present arrangements. But you are really going to need those breaks, as I am sure you are beginning to realise. The thing, though, which needs building into your planning for these sojourns, is that you are going to need management cover while you are away: someone is going to have to be employed who will be able to place orders with suppliers and sort out any and all day-to-day problems in your absence. There are agencies to supply such relief managers, and indeed it is no bad idea to employ one in your first few weeks in the job while you get settled, but don't forget they cost extra wages.

So, while I am jumping ahead of myself, do get the staff on side at the earliest opportunity and weed out any you don't feel are right after you move in. And do take holidays, but plan on the extra expense of a relief well in advance.

Mission Planning and
The Mission Statement

It is one of those dreadful words of modern management-speak, but perhaps now is the time to plan the mission, and commit pen to paper or better still fingers to word processor keyboard, and write down what you want to achieve, how you are going to get there, how you are going to fund the mission, what income you need to derive (by accounting for all your domestic outgoings), and, very importantly, any limitations or restrictions that need to be observed en route. This Mission Statement will form an integral part of your thinking, planning and doing over the next few months, and having been thrashed out with your partner and mutually agreed to be The Chosen Path, it should remain inviolate, at least for the greater part. If something comes along in the coming weeks which goes against what you have written here, then it should be considered with extra care, and the implications fully assessed, before the new arising is locked into the decision-making process. If you set out with a firmly expressed idea of what you want, and what you can and cannot do on the way to that goal, you are far more likely to achieve success than if you simply set out with hope and not much else. A serious long-distance walker would not leave home without the route marked on a suitable map, two compasses, the right clothing, nourishment and a place marked 'this pub for lunch, day one'. Treat the route to your new lifestyle in much the same way!!

Act 2

WHAT IS THE RIGHT PUB FOR YOU – LOCATION, LOCATION, LOCATION

The scene is set in the house depicted in Act One, and also in various offices and public houses around Great Britain.

OVERTURE

Taking the process to the next stage, you have by now spent months, perhaps years, dreaming of running that idyllic pub when you retire or as a second career, or, indeed even as a first if you are lucky enough to have the wherewithal while you are young enough to have the requisite energy! And as the time when you can make the change has approached you have been giving more and more thought to the practicalities. After a great deal of heartsearching and long discussions with your partner about every aspect, not to mention the onerous hardship of visiting a great many pubs at different times to assess the atmosphere and business, you are now sure you have the right relationship and the drive, energy and determination to take on The New Challenge. OK, so now you have to find a pub to run.

You now need to do four things in parallel, and not be tempted away from The Chosen Path by the rose-tinted view of the good points while the bad points are sidelined as "not really a problem."

Those three things are:

- Decide the type and location of your desired pub.
- Obtain the services of excellent, honest and trustworthy advisers.
- Obtain training both in the classroom and behind the bar.

Consider and process the method by which you are going to move from your present job and home to the new pub – all the usual house-buying traumas apply, with the added complications of having to raise finance to buy a business and make a smooth changeover so that the customers don't notice Old Jack has gone until it is too late!

SCENE ONE:

LOCATION, TYPE AND BREWERY TIES

The three types of location

Pubs fall into three basic geographic categories, although of course there are overlaps, and three distinct ownership types. You need to be very clear as to which type in either category is for you, or your decision-making will be muddied by too much choice. There are also distinct types of trade, which are referred to throughout the industry: most themed pubs fall into one of these but privately-run ones may have a mixture..

The categories of pubs are, loosely speaking: town-centre; urban/ community; and village local/rural.

Town-centre pubs attract, obviously, shoppers and tourists, according to the type of town, along with students, if it is near a university or college, and local office workers. They will typically be busiest at lunchtimes, and in non-tourist areas may not need to open on Sundays. But...

Town centres are becoming the battleground of the various large pub chains, with groups such as JD Wetherspoon and Yates's Wine Lodge having transformed, for good or bad, many towns in the mid-1990s with the opening of their highly-popular branded outlets. Is this a good thing for the privately-run pub? Yes and no seems to be the answer. Take my home town, Bury in Greater Manchester, for example. Two or three years ago it was dead at nights, with the handful of town-centre pubs doing only modest trade and having, with due respect, fairly low standards. Along comes JD Wetherspoon, Yates's and O'Neill's, all within a year and a couple of hundred yards, and all extremely smart and professional operations. The town is transformed, with hundreds of late-night drinkers being controlled by teams of "door attendants" and teams of police patrolling the streets in fortified vehicles. The result is a far more vibrant town and, interestingly, more trade for the traditional pubs and wine bars. People come into Bury on the back of the publicity for these new-style pubs, and then gradually move on to the established ones for a change – and the established pubs have nearly all been refurbished to meet the challenge, with great strides having been made to deter "undesirable" customers.

So, if you feel 'town-centre' is for you, you need to be able to cope with and cater for the likely clientele and be very aware of the present and future competition from the chains. It may well be that the oak-beamed 16th century coaching house on the High Street with a £300,000 turnover is really for sale because Old Jack has had wind of the O'Neill's coming next door in two years' time and wants out in a hurry!

Community pubs are a different kettle of fish altogether. Whether on new estates or in areas of older housing, they cater for the local population, the vast majority of customers being those who can walk in and stagger out. You may be empty at lunchtimes, when everyone is out at work, but bursting at the doors, like *The Rover's Return, Coronation Street*, as soon as the factory hooter goes, or at 10.30 of a Saturday night. The main competition here is from the growing trend to drink at home, whether home brew or branded products. And the present massive inflow of beers from Europe "for private use" in large vans is a real problem for this kind of pub in particular. Clearly, many of those who can lay hands on imported cans at under £1 are going to stay at home and watch the TV rather than wander down to your pub at £1.40 or more a pint.

> (**Sidenote:** *all prices in this book are based on those in urban Greater Manchester in mid-1998, where good beer can be had for £1.35 or even less, a pint, including foaming head!! While writing this book I made a rare visit to central London and was staggered to be charged £2.06 for a pint of cooking*

bitter, with no head, in a very ordinary "male boozer" pub. The high price reflects, of course, the higher wages 'down south', higher rents and local taxes, and the higher wholesale prices charged by the brewers, who realise people with higher wages can pay higher prices, a neat vicious spiral!! When, later on in this book, you come to work out your gross takings and profit margins, do take account of the locally-prevailing costs and prices.)

And if you feel you are the sort to run a community pub, with the emphasis on karaoke, satellite TV, Quiz Nights and the like – all good stuff and the very heart of such operations – then you need to be very aware of local fashions, traditions and the possibility of the clothing factory round the corner closing with the loss of 1000 jobs and a large part of your income.

Village and Rural is the category that most new-comers may well be attracted to. The idea of those roses climbing up the wall, the river running by, Owd Tom sitting in his corner supping a half Gill accompanied by trusty Meg (either his dog or his wife, but probably the former!) is many people's ideal. Small villages are unlikely to be invaded by the big chains, and rural areas are unlikely to see planning permission granted for a totally new pub, so your competition is far easier to judge.

But, of course, for the bulk of your trade you will be dependent on the whims of tourists, Owd Tom's halves will not keep you going, and you need to ride the success of the local attractions, the ruined abbey, the canal wharf, the long distance footpath or the Theme Park. We were once sitting in a pub we very much hoped to buy, totally alone at lunchtime and thinking that when we moved in we would have to get used to this solitude, when in walked a party of almost 30 ramblers, all wanting beer and a cooked lunch. That was a challenge! In a village/rural pub you will need to cater for parties, coaches and kids, offer excellent food at the drop of a hat and build up "drive out" trade from miles around. And, just to keep you on your toes, you may well only make a profit in the summer months, so you will view the approach of the first caravans at Easter with unaccustomed glee and anticipation....

A major factor to consider whatever the location you choose is what effect future government legislation, whether enacted or simply

And the present massive inflow of beers from Europe "for private use".

imposed by instructing the police to concentrate on different aspects of existing laws, will have. At the time of writing there is considerable talk that the "drink-driving" limits are to be reduced to "bring us into line with Europe", and while no-one would condone anyone driving having drunk alcohol to an extent that it affected their performance in any way, publicans nationwide seem to be up in arms about the proposed changes, even though, the cynic would note, they often make far more profit out of a pint of orange-and-lemonade than they do out of a pint of beer! Will a reduction in the drink-drive limit really affect sales at remote country pubs, will people stay at home more or will they walk to their local instead of driving, or will long-distance all-night taxis flourish? In many pubs the laws concerning children are openly flouted in the drive to get more trade through the doors (happily forgetting the silent many who go to pubs to get away from other people's children) and who knows, one day the government, or just the local police, may decide to apply these laws more rigidly – would this affect the type of pub you think you want? (It only takes a childless teetotal Superintendent to take over the local police division for the emphasis to change overnight from, say, anti-speeding blitzes against motorists on a particular fast road to looking closely at the degree of law-abiding in the pubs in the area.) As the nanny state seeks to protect citizens from themselves more and more, you need to be aware of the likely changes on your future livelihood.

Handy Tip Two

Pub law is, shall we say, interesting to the point of absurdity in many areas. You may not offer a drink to a person you believe to be a police officer on duty, whether in uniform or not and whether he pays or it is free. But you may offer a drink to an on-duty constable if he is accompanied by a sergeant or other more senior officer, if that senior officer approves of you so doing at the time. But you may not offer the sergeant a drink without his superior officer's express permission. It is not clear how the Chief Constable can get a drink while on duty.

(Licensing law is continually changing in both the letter and the application. In Scotland it is different from that in England and Wales, and it is different again in Ireland and in Europe. References to law in this book are for guidance and illustration, and should not be taken as authoritative.)

Of course, not all pubs fall exactly into these categories, and as with everything there are shades of grey, but you need to decide which type is best for your circumstances and character. If you were born

Owd Tom's halves will not keep you going.

and bred in inner London, you might not fit in well in the heart of the Dales, and vice versa. But you might thrive on the change, only you and your partner can tell, although the locals will soon confirm, or otherwise, your decision.

Type of ownership

You then need to decide which type of pub is for you, as far as the pub's ownership and operation is concerned, and this is largely a question of the capital you have available. Leaving aside actually working for a pub-operator as an employee in a chain such as Yates's, the three types are managed, leased (tenanted) and freehold.

In a managed pub you are, either in effect or in fact, the employee of the brewery or pub-operator that owns the building. You sell their products at their prices and offer the type of operation they want to have. Brewery specialist staff help you achieve your targets – you will be given all the appropriate training and guidance as to how to reach the goals and set the required atmosphere and standards – and the profits are theirs at the end of the day; you have a wage just like any employee, or you might be self-employed and take out a regular fee, but either way you are in the grasp of the brewery. You usually buy the fixtures and fittings and glassware from the previous owner, and sell them on when you leave, and you may well have to put up a bond to the brewery as a sign of goodwill and to guard against you deserting the ship with the takings, but you may be able to move in and take over for very little outlay indeed, especially if the brewery wants rid of the outgoing landlord or he has "left" the place is actually standing empty. With this type of operation there is the least amount of commitment, and, although you may lose your bond and the money you paid for the glasses etc., if you hate it you can simply hand back the keys.

Such pubs are usually in urban or suburban locations, and these days are often themed or branded, but they offer a way into the trade at very low cost and with only a minimal degree of "own boss" style of working.

A leased pub is the way if you have moderate capital to invest and don't mind the fact that the brewery will rule you to a certain (large) extent! Most leased pubs are owned by a brewery or pub-owning chain such as Inntrepreneur, although a few, and these in my opinion are far more desirable, are owned by private landlords or companies not connected with brewing, perhaps even the local council.

Depending on its location and turnover, a lease will cost from a few thousand pounds to £100,000 or even more. On top of this you will pay for the fixtures and fittings and glasses, at an agreed price, and, as with any pub purchase, the value of the 'wet and dry' stock (that is drinks and food) on the day of changeover, the so-called 'stock at valuation' (SAV).

Pub leases used to vary widely between breweries but are now becoming more and more uniform. They generally run for 15 or 20 years, from a start date some time in the past, not from the date when you take over unless you can negotiate a new lease, so the price you pay also depends on the number of years remaining.

Clearly there is a big point to watch here. If, for example, you are considering a pub with a 15-year lease but which has only seven years to go, then in five years' time, when you might, for the sake of argument, be likely to either retire or move on to something more challenging, there will be only two years to go on the lease. At this point the lease will be almost unsaleable, unless the owner (i.e. the brewery) is willing to offer a brand new lease to the incoming owner. So, your expenditure of, say, £75,000 on the lease and goodwill now will gradually dwindle over the years as the lease runs down.

Equally, while you have security of tenure during the lifetime of the lease, in much the same way as you would if you were renting a private dwelling, when the lease expires you could be out on the streets. If, for example, the owner wants to put in a nominated tenant, or change the pub into a club and rebuild it, or whatever, at the end of the lease if it is not willing to offer you a new one that is the end of your business, and all you have striven to build up. So be very careful about the length of time a lease has to run in relation to the time you intend staying there, and think very hard before taking on anything with less than, say, ten years' lease left.

But one of the biggest lessons we learned while pub-hunting was regarding rent reviews.

Innocents, as we were, might think that brewery-landlords would want to see their leaseholders flourish and that they might reward good performance, not penalise it. Part of the "deal" when buying a leasehold pub is that you not only pay the landlord rent, but also are tied to that brewery's beer – no big thing, you might think, as the major breweries all have a wide range of beers these days, and legislation forces the big national breweries to allow you one "guest" ale: a draught beer not on their normal sales list.

However, rents are reviewed sometimes every three years, in other leases every five, and, while in theory you can appeal against a seemingly unfairly large hike in rent in practice, this appeals procedure will not get you very far, and it may cost you dearly in fees, time and nervous energy. In any case, when it comes to reviews the breweries don't sit down and say, "now, you are a very good landlord and are selling lots of our beer, so we will not raise your rent this time", they, in general, always go in on the attack, determined to squeeze every penny out of the landlord, who, as he is obliged to pay the rent until he can find someone to buy the lease from him, is effectively trapped. It is more a case of, "now, you are a very good landlord and are selling lots more of our beer, so you are making extra profit, which we want in the form of extra rent." The landlord cannot say to the brewery, "I am not paying that ludicrous rent, stuff your pub," – he has to find a buyer to pay the rent until changeover day. The breweries know this, of course, but there are still so many folk queuing to buy good leaseholds that they can get away with being aggressive and money-grabbing rather than committing themselves to growing and developing a pub's overall business.

The rent might be, for the sake of argument, £30,000 a year and the brewery might write to you saying it is raising it to £40,000 at the next review – there is a formal procedure whereby the landlord is notified a few months in advance of the proposed review, or rise, and given the opportunity to appeal. (The dates of these reviews are set out in the lease, so you are aware of them before you sign for the pub, but the size of the rise depends largely on what trade the brewery thinks you are doing, that is they take account of your perceived profit.)

You are expected to fight, for this is an adversarial relationship, and it might be conceded that the rise will be £500 or £1000 a year less than initially proposed: but, of course, such reduction was built into the original demand anyway. If you accept the proposed rise without complaint you will be taken as a soft touch and can expect more of the same next time round. If you appeal, it will cost you time and money and is hardly worth the effort in terms of the reduction you will get. Coming from a very different industry this aggressive attitude towards a customer – for that is what a landlord is – came as a great shock, and if pub landlords treated their customers the way breweries treat their landlords, there would be no pubs – all beer would be drunk at home!!

But the real shock came when we learned the size of some rises. Now, I appreciate these examples may not be typical, but of the five pubs we seriously considered buying, three were leasehold, and two of those had had rent rises of over two-thirds in the past year. Imagine trading in a pub, doing your best and slowly building up trade, but even so scraping hard to pay the bills, and the brewery comes along and says "right, Mr Smith, your rent from next September will be going up by £10,000 a year." That, of course, will make your pub almost unviable and I have no doubt that the two pubs we looked at were being sold largely because the landlords could not sensibly afford the increased rent. So beware: while renting a pub is a good way to get started with a modest outlay, rent rises can be huge, and there is little chance, if any, of you being able to negotiate a meaningful amelioration. If you do well and sell more beer the brewery will take more rent: if you do badly and sell less beer the brewery will still take more rent, your welfare is not its concern, unlikely any other supplier/customer relationship.

Brewery ties

As I say, as well as charging you rent, the brewery also ties you to their draught beer products, and while you will probably be free to buy bottled beers, spirits, wines and soft drinks from whom you please, having to take their beer gives the brewery another huge advantage: they can calculate fairly accurately from the amount of beer purchased from them what your gross takings are, and thus what your profit is (or should be) and from that what rent you can "afford". And, as you are legally tied to those supplies, they can also charge effectively what they like for the beers they do sell you.

It certainly came as a surprise to us when we started looking at leasing a pub that there are two price lists for beers from a brewery:

the sales list price, typically around £220 (excluding VAT) for a 36-gallon barrel, which applies to tied houses and to one-off sales (if someone wanted a barrel for a party or something like that), and the price charged to "free" houses – those freehold pubs and pubs rented from private owners which are not breweries – who are able to negotiate their prices with any supplier they choose. Again typically, a brewery will offer a £60 a barrel discount – that's 21 pence a pint – to a free house compared with the tied price, the price a tied leaseholder has to accept for his draught beer supplies. That 21p, as we shall see when I discuss finance, makes a huge difference to the profitability of a pub. (Although beer is never supplied in barrels as large as 36 gallons, since no-one could lift it, "a barrel" always means 36 gallons unless otherwise stated. Breweries sell beer (in 1998) from around £190 a barrel for ordinary bitter to almost £300 a barrel for premium lager, and prices vary from region to region for the same product.)

So, when thinking of a lease, yes, it enables you to get started with modest outlay and be your own boss. The good news about a lease is that, unlike a tenancy where you have less freedom, as long as you don't contravene the terms of the lease, which are not onerous, and pay the rent properly, you can run the pub as you wish, theme it as you wish and target whatever sort of customers you wish. Nude karaoke or chapel hymn singing every night will not bother the brewery!! On the other hand, the rent will be way above what a private landlord will charge, and it may rise dramatically every three or five years (it can actually rise every year, in three or five year cycles) and you will be charged £60 a barrel more than the free house down the road is being charged for the same beer off the same delivery wagon.

As a personal statement, I have to say that while many landlords seem to want to winge about Britain's strange opening hours and laws regarding children and licensed areas, a far bigger problem for the industry is the attitude of breweries, and it staggers us that the policies and practices we came across, which, we are told, are quite the industry standards, are legal. I think the philosophy stems from a belief that many/some/most landlords are on some sort of fiddle, buying in beer secretly which breaks the tie, taking cash out of the till without accounting for it, or fiddles we never got as far as learning, and therefore the breweries act on the assumption that you are one of those, regardless of who or what you are. And so, if you are being

Nude karaoke or chapel hymn singing every night will not bother the brewery!!

tarred with a brush marked "dishonest" or "untrustworthy", there is no incentive for you to be otherwise, as, once again, will be seen when I turn to finance.

From our personal point of view, leasing from a brewery was not an acceptable way of life, but leasing from a private owner, if you can find such a pub, would seem to be ideal. They do exist, and from what we have seen rents are one third those of brewery houses, and, of course, you can sell whose beer you choose. (Such pubs are often owned either by a local council, by a small chain – although these can be tied – or an individual, or even by a freehold landlord who does not want to sell his own pub but wants to rent it out for steady income and capital growth reasons.)

To go into this tie arrangement in a little more depth. It applies only to the big national breweries, such as Scottish & Newcastle (S&N), Whitbread, Bass (which now has very few leased houses), and Allied Domecq (a part of Carlsberg-Tetley). It does not apply to leases from pub-leasing chains, who can tie you totally to their nominated brands, nor to smaller breweries.

But if you lease from what is termed a "Big Brewer", your lease will include clauses on the lines of the following, in long-winded legalese, of course:

- you must buy all your beer from the brewery's nominated depot or supplier, as the brewery shall dictate.

- you will pay the full price as shown on the price list the brewery will supply.

- you will not "sell or expose for sale or bring on to the premises for the purposes of sale (I love that clause!) any beer which is not on the brewery's list or is not supplied by the brewery.

- except that "the tenant has the right to purchase from whosoever he chooses one brand of cask-conditioned beer selected by him, and to sell or expose the same for sale on the premises".

But do note that these provisions exclude bottled and canned beers, and also all wines, spirits and soft drinks: a brewery tie only extends to draught beers, lagers and stouts, which will account for perhaps one-third of your drinks sales.

While some people might think the idea is to allow the landlord to sell a "real ale" from a small producer, and thus allow greater choice on his bar and access to the big breweries' pubs for the little brewer, while this is true it is not the main effect as far as the landlord is concerned, largely because the big brewers offer beer from nominated small ones as part of the tie, and also because there is a practical limit to the number of different beers you can actually sell: cellar and bar space being two determinants, and cask life being the third.

Allied Domecq/Carlsberg-Tetley is a case in point. Its "tied" beers include such brands as Tetley, Burton, Green King, Greenalls, Kilkenny and Marstons beers, Guinness stout, and Carlsberg, Skol and Labbatt's lagers, but the brewery also offers a rotating choice of "real ales" from small breweries, the beers under this "Tapster's Choice" scheme rotating every week over a six-month period from a nationwide list of some 18.

Similarly, Bass-leased pubs are tied to brands which include Bass, Stones', Tennant's, Caffreys, Worthington, Carling and Guinness. But Bass has a "Cask Masters" range of brands from other breweries: these beers are more from mid-sized regional breweries such as Thwaites and Robinsons, compared to the specialist beers offered by Carlsberg-Tetley. Whitbread (Boddingtons, Flowers, Castle Eden, Thwaites, Heineken etc.) and S&N (Younger's, John Smith's, McEwan's, Courage, Theakston's and, of course, Newcastle Brown) have similar broad based ranges of products within the tie, so the tie itself – at least in terms of product choice and variety – is not as onerous as it might seem on first sight.

So, regardless of which "big brewer" the landlord is tied to, there is more than enough choice of popular brands and guest ales to happily fill any bar and any cellar, and it might be foolish to use up the "Guest Ale Provision" with another specialist beer which will only sell slowly to particular customers. All the above beers are sold to the leasehold landlord at the full list price, take it or leave it, but by buying the "guest ale" from another major brewery or independent supplier (and you will have no shortage of sales reps trying hard to sell you their wares in this respect!!), the above-mentioned discount of around £60 a barrel can be obtained, so it is wise to use this "freedom" to have a highly-popular mainstream brand which will sell at least as well as the tied brands and on which you can make the extra profit.

For example, if you are a Carlsberg-Tetley house surrounded by other C-T pubs all selling Tetley beer, you might find Boddingtons sells well as a way of giving customers a change from their usual, and as you will be able to buy it for 20 pence or more less than you pay for the "tied" Tetley's beer – and it should sell well, being a very well-known, highly-publicised brand.

Or the other way round, if you are a Bass pub in the middle of C-T country, you can buy in Tetley beer as your guest ale far cheaper than the pub next door gets its "tied" beer from C-T, and thus you can happily undercut him by 10p a pint, sell more beer, all other things being equal, and make 10p+ more profit on each pint. That is how daft the whole idea of ties and guest beer is, which reflects on the people who maintain this antiquated way of doing business.

Of course, it is not unknown for some landlords to cheat the system. As I said before, breweries expect landlords to fiddle as much as they can and some landlords have an almost cat and mouse running battle with their brewery-masters. Simple things like this are, shall we say, well-known, but, faced with having to buy brands which are not popular locally at the full list price, a landlord might buy two guest ales from his independent supplier, and then "simply" cover over one of the beer-pump labels when any brewery employee is detected arriving in the car park. Or he may buy in more barrels of his tied beer from an independent supplier, so he gets the discount on a part of his "allowed" supplies, AND can still have a popular and discounted guest ale as well. Of course you can expect your Area Manager to get Very Cross if he detects anything as basic as this...

The big four brewers, from time to time, change their emphasis as to whether they want to operate or own pubs, and if so how and where. So, one day one of them will sell hundreds of its leased pubs to a chain, thinking that leasehold operations are not where it wants to be, while another day another brewer will buy a lot of pubs and turn them into managed branded outlets. In 1997, for example, Bass sold most of its leased pubs to a Japanese-owned company, while S&N bought branded pubs and "released to the market" some tied leased pubs so as to best pursue its own corporate philosophy.

...and then "simply" cover over one of the beer-pump labels when any brewery employee is detected arriving in the car park.

These games for the big boys do not really concern you, except that it is useful to know the way the large companies are thinking. If, for the sake of this argument, one or two of the big four are moving towards managed and branded pubs and away from leased ones, there must be a reason, and that may well be that they see more profit for their shareholders with that particular balance within their operations. If your local town centre suddenly has a JD Wetherspoon, a Yates's and a branded brewery outlet such as a Rat and Parrot, then again it is a sign the world is turning. In general it does seem to be the trend that the big operators are moving more towards themed and branded managed houses, while little operators are growing up all the time, and buying up freeholds to turn into leased or managed houses under their control. As with many industries you might conclude that the little man, the sole trader, is being squeezed, or bought out.

As we have never had dealings with S&N, and therefore cannot comment at all on their ways of doing business, I feel I can relate directly some facts found on the company's own web site on the Internet.

> "The company has an estate of over 2000 managed and tenanted sites throughout the country. More than 70% of the estate is made up of managed houses. S&N outlets enjoy the highest profitability in the industry. A graphic indicates that the profit per managed outlet rose from £58,000 to £79,000 between 1995 and 1997. An increasing proportion of the estate is branded, a trend which will continue. Another graphic shows 21% of the estate was branded, and the target for the year 2000 is 54%. S&N's brands include Rat & Parrot, Old Orleans and Chef & Brewer. In 1996/97 the company invested £116 million in real estate; profits of the pub and restaurant division increased by 9% to £171.6 million. Scottish Courage (the brewing division) is the leading brewer in the UK and has a 28% wholesale share of the UK beer market."

> The website (these quotes were taken in May 1998) also notes that "28% of the estate (about 700 pubs) is comprised of tenancies (which tend to be the lowest profit per site outlets). This is well below our competitors: Whitbread has 56%, Allied Domecq (effectively the tenant arm of Carlsberg-Tetley) 45% and Bass 35%".

All sorts of inferences can be drawn from these simple sentences.

Handy Tip Three

There is a wealth of information on every conceivable subject on the Internet, as well as well over 20,000 newsgroups where you can post information or ask questions on an equally wide range of subjects. While much of the information is officially placed on the net by the particular company, there is a great deal of unofficial information and gossip. Spend an evening or two "surfing the net" and you will be amazed at what you find out about pubs, the licensed trade or any aspect of any topic you care to name. A very good investment, if you have not already done so, at this early stage in your deliberations when you need all the information you can get.

The S&N website also has information on its tenancies:

> *"The S&N Partnership Package has been designed to present the right balance of support and freedom to enable tenants to build successful businesses. S&N is the first national pub retailer to develop three year lease agreements (five in Scotland). The innovative lease has been developed primarily with the publican in mind. S&N also provides an attractive low-cost entry agreement which allows prospective tenants who may not have the capital necessary for most standard leases to start a partnership business."*

Handy Tip Four

If you decide a leased pub is the choice for you, what will you do if you hate it after six months, or if your partner is taken ill and you can't cope on your own, or some other catastrophe occurs and you need to sell up? Make sure at an early stage in your interest in any specific leased pub if you are tied by the lease to remaining leaseholders for a set minimum time, and if so what the penalties are if you feel compelled to sell early.

I am sure many other brewers and pub operators have equally excellent websites with lots of useful information. I have deliberately only quoted the S&N one as it is the only one of the four "big brewers" we have not had direct dealings with, and therefore I have not been tempted to put any "personal flavourings" into the above quotes and commentary.

Freehold pubs

For many would-be landlords these are ideal, since you are your own boss, owe no allegiance to anyone (except perhaps the bank manager) and are free to do what you please when you please, within the strictures of the law, of course. You can buy your beer from whichever company, brewery or independent supplier, you choose, when you choose. You can offer for sale beers from all four of the "Big Brewers", any of them or none at all. You can change the brands you offer as often as you please, which will confuse your regulars, who won't be for long, or never, which might become boring. The choice is yours, giving you total business freedom. Your fate is in your hands!!

The problem is one of capital. As a rule of thumb, (and it applies well in the north of England where we were doing our research, and from what we saw there is very little difference across the country, unlike private dwelling houses where southern prices are much higher than the north), the cost of a freehold pub is £90,000 plus the annual takings net of VAT. Thus a pub with annual takings of £150,000, from which you ought to be able to derive an income before tax of around £30,000 without any 'fiddling the books', will sell for around £240,000, give or take all the usual caveats. On the other hand, a leasehold pub taking over £300,000 (which will give you a comparable income) a year and with, say, 15 years of the lease left, may cost less than £100,000, but then you have the rent and higher beer prices to find. It is an interesting sideline that in the south of England, where pub trade has been hit hard by the "personal" importation of van loads of beer from across The Channel at low prices, pubs have been sold off for this "£90,000 plus turnover" type of price and then closed by the new owners and converted into purely domestic accommodation which is immediately worth far more than the purchase price!!

If you have a quarter of a million to invest in a new business venture, then this seems a reasonable way to do it. If you have to borrow some of the capital or don't want to risk all your nest egg, then you need to think carefully. Freehold pubs come on the market at prices well over £300,000, reflecting much higher turnover, but I would suggest that something in the £200,000 to £250,000 bracket will give you the size of business you can handle as newcomers to the industry, without too many staff or large scale facilities, while still providing a livable income.

It is also worth noting that many good freehold pubs are snapped up by brewery or pub-operating chains at inflated prices as soon as they come on the market. Naturally you want to buy a good pub, but freehold ones of quality are becoming scarcer to find. If you find a "gem" you may also find yourself battling with the very large cheque book of a plc.

In summary, then, a managed pub offers a very cheap way in, most probably in an urban or suburban area. While you are your own boss in many respects, you are employed by and heavily tied to the brewery, and have very little room for "self expression": the brewery will almost set the theme it wants the pub to be, and if you don't like the resultant atmosphere or type of trade that is just tough!!

A leasehold (tenanted) pub offers more freedom, but the restrictions of tied draught beer supplies (at a fixed, high price) and a very heavy rent which will be reviewed at regular intervals – upwards, and possibly dramatically, especially if you have been successful in increasing trade – may deter you. But you have security and very little interference from the brewery unless you default on the rent or do something stupid, or illegal.

A free-of-tie lease offers the same plusses but with the added advantage of being able to choose your beer supplier, from whom you can negotiate a good discount. The rent should also be lower.

A freehold pub means no rent and the discount of "free choice" beer supplies, but to get a sensible profit level you will need a capital outlay of around a quarter of a million pounds or even more. You can also choose your own decor or theme, and chase the type of customer you want in your pub, regardless of whether that will give you the maximum profit.

· ·

The right pub –
location, location, location, again

You now have a clear idea of what category of pub is for you – town-centre, community or village/rural, and what type you can afford or want to run – tenanted, leased or freehold. That enables you to narrow your target down when looking at pub-for-sale advertisements in the press or estate agents' sales details, but there is now another factor to consider: where in the country you wish to live and work?

Really for practical reasons you need to remain in your comfy armchair for the moment and discuss with your partner whereabouts you want this ideal pub to be. You might have been born and lived all your life in, say, Leeds and think, quite rightly, it is the centre of the universe and want to stay close to kith and kin by running a pub in an area where you are familiar with the geography and well known by many in the community. Or you may feel your home town is the pits of the earth and want to move to that idyllic rose-covered pub in Dorset. And any combination in between, but you do need to define your area.

The practical aspect is one of how you are going to do the research. If, to continue the example, you plan to move from Leeds to Dorset, how are you going to find out about pubs in Dorset? Yes, you can contact all the relevant estate agents, and you can even compile your own database, but you will need to visit each pub that comes on the market in the chosen area, and, when one comes up that is even vaguely "OK" make a major visit to assess it and all its competition. You need to become very familiar with the area in terms of where facilities are, any plans for major works such as by-passes and retail parks that could affect trade in a specific area, and any local gossip – for example, perhaps there is a rumour going round that a major tourist attraction which would be a significant part of your custom is about to close or expand. In our research we had a specific requirement to be close to reasonable public transport, so we needed to be aware of local rail and bus services. Other possible considerations are access, sufficient for your own personal circumstances, to your bank, church, doctor, hospital, supermarket or any other service you subconsciously rely on at the moment. If you currently visit a hospital every month for a check-up there is little point in thinking of buying a pub many miles from a comparable service.

So, while moving a long way is by no means impossible, "how you are going to do it?" needs thinking through before you start being overwhelmed by estate agents' details.

Handy Tip Five

Which reminds me, estate agents. More on these later, but a book we read when we were at the stage you are at now said that to find our idyllic pub all we had to do was register with estate agents and sit back and wait for details to come flooding through the letter box. That does not happen, and you will need to do a lot of leg work yourself and be prepared to be patient. The ideal pub will not arrive tomorrow!

And if you choose to stay in your present locality, again reflect on the implications. Of course if your ideal is actually your present local and you know the landlord is retiring soon and willing to sell to you, your problem is solved – although having read this far I am sure you will realise that what appears to be a superb, well-oiled, tightly-knit business opportunity might just have "interesting challenges" behind the scenes. Check, check, check, as always.

And if you are staying locally, who knows how many old friends you haven't seen for years might come crawling out of the proverbial woodwork seeking jobs or free drinks. Pubs are not the places to do favours for friends, a very easy way to go broke very fast, so set firm rules early on and make sure friends and family know there will be no "easy touches".

Type of trade – your market sector

Very briefly, the distinct types of trade for a pub are broken down into: young people; 25-45 singles; young couples; young families; grey market (50+); females alone; male boozer; safe couples; quiet local; and tourist. Any pub will attract, because of its location and reputation one, possibly two of these categories above all others. Families with young children will avoid a pub with young people's music blaring and light flashing, and vice versa. Females alone will not go into a male boozer, and more mature couples out for a night away from the family will not go into a pub full of bouncy castles. Pub chains will theme each of their pubs to attract the type of trade they see best for that outlet, and are extremely good at doing this.

You have by now decided where you want to be, what sort of location and what sort of ownership. You also have to decide whether, having found a pub which meets those fundamental criteria, it also meets, or can be changed so as to meet, the kind of market you feel you will be happiest in. If the pub you are going after is, shall we say, a quiet local, it will be hard to make it work as a young families pub. If it is a young families pub and Mega-Pubs plc has a themed families pub next door, perhaps you ought to avoid this one, unless you have the wherewithal to drastically change it and wait for it to become established in its new niche. If you hate kids, running one which is tailored for them might not be a good idea, you won't be able to relate to their needs. If you are of slight build and a pacifist nature running a male boozer on the edge of a large council estate, even if it is actually in rolling countryside, might not be a good move even if everything else stacks up.

Everyone will have their own idea of the best place to go, it might even be abroad, but the practicalities do need agreeing. Your partner might hate Dorset, even though you dream every night of the roses above the door: or he or she might not have had the privilege of being born in God's Own County and be pining for a move back to Norfolk, Pembroke or the Shetlands – how will you keep up with your friends in such a strange, to you, area? The short answer is you won't – in pubs there is little time to keep up with the past!

So, get a large map of the World, Europe, the UK, or England, Scotland, Wales or Ireland, according to where your greater boundaries of aspiration lie, and sit down again with your partner and cross through areas either of you does not want to move to until you are left with ideally one, but maybe two zones of mutual agreement. From experience, and assuming you are staying in the UK, if this area covers 50-60 miles square it will yield enough pubs and enough running about to keep you happy for quite a few weeks! Having done this you have decided on one aspect of the most important aspect of the whole pub-selecting and buying process – Location, Location, LOCATION.

You are now at the end of Part One of the task of finding The Pub, a part which has involved little more than sitting comfortably and

If the pub you are going after is, shall we say, a quiet local, it will be hard to make it work as a young families pub.

thinking hard and talking earnestly with the likes of your partner, friends and family and as many serving and former landlords as will listen. Before moving to Part Two, get all the advice you can, study all the angles and, finally, get yourself the *Yellow Pages* or comparable trade directories for your chosen area, and the relevant Ordnance Survey Landranger sheets and local town street plans. You have thought long and hard and talked it over incessantly. You have earned a drink!!

Coincidental Footnote 1

By one of those strange coincidences, on the very day that these words were being consigned to the word processor, in May 1998, the local weekly paper carried the following Page One lead story, under the headline "Bull Fight". I quote verbatim, except for keeping the name of the pub, and its landlord anonymous.

"Former Royal Marine Mr X spent his life savings ridding a town centre pub of its "drug den" reputation. Now he says the brewery has repaid him by ordering him out of the pub.

The brewery says the landlord owes £4000 in rent: he says he was promised help by the brewery. He has spent £30,000 cleaning up the pub and he wants the money back before he goes.

The landlord has been told to leave the pub by next Friday. He will be penniless and homeless. He says his wife and children left him because of the stress.

The tough ex-soldier took over the pub in February of last year and fulfilled his promise to rid it of drugs and under-age drinkers. Customers returned and (I presume weekly) takings are up from £900 to more than £3000 in the first quarter of this year.

However, the landlord claims that the brewery has gone back on promises of support when he and his wife were taken on as troubleshooters. The owners have now issued a termination of agreement notice due to spiralling rent arrears.

The row between the landlord and the brewery surrounds promises about rent payments which he says were made by an employee of the brewery who has since left the company.

As well as clearing out undesirables in his 15 months there, the landlord installed a modern kitchen, a 24-seat restaurant and says he has worked virtually without pay or leave in order to ensure the success of the pub.

'I have worked very hard and ploughed all my life savings to revitalise the pub. And this is how the brewery repay me, by evicting me from the premises without any financial return whatsoever,' said a bitter landlord.

'The pressures placed on me and my family have been intolerable. I have lost my wife and children because of it.'

The Business Development Manager of the brewery, based in Blackburn, refused to comment on the matter except to say that the 'eviction notice' was a termination of agreement notice in line with the landlord's current contract."

* The following week the local paper reported that the landlord was barricading himself in the domestic accommodation, going on hunger strike and putting banners on the outside of the pub proclaiming his grievance. He was also reported as saying he would refuse to hand back his licence to the brewery. The brewery said nuffin.

Apart from the relevance of this story to my own thoughts expressed above, readers may also note how breweries' apparent promises can seemingly be over-ruled or circumvented, after they have read of our experiences with another brewery outlined in the following section. The pub re-opened a few weeks later, and a couple of months later on the landlord had a heart attack.

Coincidental Footnote 2

Also while writing these words, an estate agent's sales leaflet arrived in the post for a pub which is in one of my very favourite market towns. It illustrates well the difference between privately-leased and brewery-leased pubs, and the difficulties of making a living in rural outlets.

Uniquely in our experience, this pub is offered either as leasehold, for £45,000, or freehold, at £180,000. The turnover is given as just under £100,000, with only 20% coming from food and 10% from accommodation. Compared with what we saw to be a typical brewery rent of £30,000+ a year, this pub is offered with a new three-year lease at just £12,000, with an option to buy at the end of that time. Yet the profit after rent is just £13,000. Potential perhaps, a lovely location certainly, but not riches!

Handy Tips Six, Seven and Eight

The job title "Business Development Manager" means the holder is charged with developing the brewery's business, not the landlord's.

The use of such words as "Partnership" might not always mean the literal dictionary definition of the word.

If a brewery employee of whatever status makes a statement regarding any financial or contractual matter – a loan, an interest rate, a period of repayment or whatever – do not take any notice of it until it is in writing and accepted as a valid undertaking by your solicitor or professional adviser. It is, I am told, the standard practice of breweries for a junior manager to be told to make an offer to "get you hooked" and then for that offer to be flatly denied once you have signed up, and for the person who made the offer to have "left the company" when you complain about the seeming deception.

To accommodate or not...

Many rural and country town pubs offer accommodation, and with the growth in tourism this is seen as a good thing to offer – "this is the easy money" one landlady told us. Now, while offering B&B to visitors may bring in welcome extra trade, there is, of course, legislation which might affect your plans, not least fire regulations where they apply. However, within the remit of this book it is worthwhile considering before you look too deeply into a pub offering accommodation whether the financial rewards are worth the effort. A pub anyway will tie you up from, say, 9am to after 11pm every day, but those staying with you will want a cooked breakfast at perhaps 7.30 or 8.00, requiring a much earlier start, and may also feel the need for a drink long after closing time. Your long day is longer, and you have the laundry to look after, and extra marketing costs. All that for perhaps £25 a night?

The use of such words as "Partnership" might not always mean the literal dictionary definition of the word.

End of Part One
Ten-Point Check List

This is a suitable place to pause and reflect – before proceeding, you should have safely passed all these Check Points.

1 Is your relationship right? Do you both want to run a pub and are you both agreed absolutely on the division of work?

2 Are there any family implications? Children, ageing relatives or even pets to consider?

3 Do you both have the energy and enthusiasm for a 100+ hours a week commitment, honestly?

4 Are you sure what category of pub you want – town-centre, community or village/rural?

5 ...and what type – tenanted, leased or freehold?

6 ...and in what locality?

7 Does the life of a landlord suit you both? The crowded Saturday nights and lonely Monday lunchtimes, karaoke or lunches for the rambling club. Are you happy on a personal basis with the ethos of pubs and breweries, with the concept of a tie, of the present and likely future licensing laws and of responsibilities in such areas as drunkenness, violence and drugs?

8 Have you given any thought to how you are going to give up your present job(s) and move to being a publican?

9 Have you the money in the bank to be able to buy the type and category of pub you want, or are you going to have to borrow, even short term to make the move?

10 And above all, do 1-9 again and ask yourself while sober and standing under a cold shower, am I sure I want to be a landlord??? It is a big commitment, especially if you are middle-aged and seeking a second career in new surroundings, and you need to be 101% sure, like we thought we were, before you spend any money!

SCENE TWO:

GET THE BEST ADVICE

The scene is largely set in the offices of various advisers, and in selected pubs in your chosen area.

If you are still moving ahead with your plan, you now need to start doing more tasks in parallel, and pub-finding-and-buying will start to take over your lives.

Most importantly, you will need to surround yourselves with the best possible advisers, and acquire the most comprehensive information as to what pubs are on the market in your selected area of the country. You will also have to undergo a considerable amount of training, pass exams and get hands-on experience.

The two main advisers you will have to retain at an early stage are a solicitor and an accountant. If you currently run a business or are of some financial status you may already have both, but if you are in a full-time job and have only ever used a solicitor to move house years ago, you may want to look around.

While the people whom we came into contact with during our own nine-month pub search are remaining anonymous in this book so as to avoid, as best we can, any further recrimination from those who did us wrong, we have to say the advice we got from our solicitor and accountant were the best. As it happens, both were advisers of long-standing, which I am sure helped. The solicitors (we actually used two, with different professional skills) are both partners in small firms and the accountant is a sole-trader: that means they give more personal service and have lower overheads to pass on to their clients. We got the very best of service at most modest prices from both. Huge offices, glittering foyers and 7-series BMWs do not necessarily mean better service, better advice or easier access, and someone has to pay for those frills. (Personally I would never use an adviser who arrived at my door in a 7-series. He is, almost by definition, charging too much for his time and he is immodest enough not to realise it!)

If you don't have a good accountant or solicitor, ask around for personal recommendations. Visit a few and outline your needs and

· ·

assess their capabilities, experience and scale of charges, and make sure that the person you see will be the person with whom you will have day-to-day contact. If there is any hint of your work being passed to an inexperienced junior, or if there are a set of golf clubs in the corner of the office, indicating that normal office hours are not always maintained, or if the desk is a mountain of jumbled papers, indicating a jumbled mind and a badly-managed or too heavy work load, move on. With the likelihood of a long-term association in the offing, rather than just the one-off transaction of a house conveyance, most should offer you a good rate and be able to express some knowledge of the licensed trade. Nevertheless, even the most humble solicitor is going to charge you at least £75 an hour – a bigger firm may reach £1000 a day or more.

Handy Tip Nine

To make £1000 profit after all dues and taxes, even in a free house in an affluent area, you need to sell some seven thousand pints of bitter.... Be careful with such expenditure.

You may decide you need to have these key advisers not in the town where you live now, but in the town you plan to move to. Your solicitor needs to be, pardon the pun, on tap, and, if legal trouble does arise, will have to be able to get to you rapidly and perhaps even attend the local court or police station. You will in any case want to have a local and experienced solicitor to handle your on-licence application when it comes before the magistrates. When we thought we were buying "Pub One" (see Strike the Set) our normal and long-established solicitor rang the Clerk to the Magistrates' Court in the relevant town and was given the name of the local solicitor whom they saw most often at the Licensing Hearings. The arrangement worked very well: our usual solicitor, who knows us and our foibles well, was able to act speedily on matters concerning the property, while the "new" solicitor brought a wealth of licensing experience and familiarity with the local system to bear, and he was within walking distance of the Magistrates' Court. Such a local solicitor will also be able to advise you on specific local matters, such as the on-the-ground attitude of police and magistrates to new landlords, under age drinking and any putative plans you might have to change the image of a particular pub. Nude karaoke will not turn a hair in some towns, in others the men in blue will be down on you before the posters go up – well almost!!

Your accountant can perhaps be a little more geographically remote, but if you plan to keep good and accurate books, as you most surely must, then it is a good idea if he visits you to go through your trading figures, prepare your VAT return and other such tasks, on a regular basis.

Some professionals place advertisements for accountancy services "tailored to the licensed trade". This usually indicates some familiarity with the many "fiddles", for want of a better word, that some landlords can get up to. You may well feel that knowledge of all these tricks of the trade will help maximise how much you can take out of the business for yourself. But also consider that when you come to sell, any astute buyer, or at least his astute accountant, will notice these ways of doing things and will amend his view of your business, and its worth, accordingly. What you fiddle today you will lose tomorrow!

You must also speak long and often to your bank, and the big advantage of this is that theirs is, essentially, advice born out of much local experience. Again, if you have a business bank account you will have a business banking manager who will give you the bank's view in general terms. But the business banking manager of the branch local to your selected area will almost certainly know of any good, or bad, points about a particular pub, and of any local issues, such as the impact of development schemes or factory closures.

It is a delicate matter of timing as to when you seek local advice; you need it, certainly, from both solicitors and bank, but remember their knowledge will be quite localised. If you plan, say, on buying a pub in Preston or Basingstoke or Bristol, but have second thoughts and end up in Lancaster, Andover or Bath, you may find yourself having to do the research all over again, or at the least having your bank branch more miles away than would be optimum. This is just one of the smaller balancing acts you are facing at this stage of your quest.

The adviser you are going to need most – and this is where we made our biggest mistake – is the consultant who can help you find the right pub, negotiate the right price, handle the changeover with skill and dexterity and then help you get established, coming back to see you on a regular basis to help you maximise business and profitability.

As I mentioned right at the beginning, today more and more people are seeking to run a pub, whether for a first or second career, and there is thus increasing competition for the good pubs that come on the market. At the same time new chains are fast-developing and existing brewery chains are changing policy. This means there are more people wanting to advise would-be newcomers to the industry, and the trade papers have advertisements from these consultants, seeking your business.

As with every step you take in business, this one no more and no less than any others, do take care to select the right consultant, one who can provide for your needs, charges a sensible rate, has the right resources to hand and with who you get on, like your solicitor and accountant, on a personal level. We thought we had taken all the right steps but were proved horribly wrong and it cost us dearly in time, money, mental health and sleep.

The first step, having telephoned each consultant on your list and talked in brief about your situation and then having received the brochure, is to have a face-to-face introductory chat.

> **Rule One – he is your consultant, so, unless there is a pressing need for you to visit his offices, he visits you, at your convenience. If he arrives very late or spends half the meeting talking on his mobile phone to other clients, agents or whatever, ask yourself if he really has the resources to handle you as well. If he arrives in a flashy car, is he charging too much? There may be hidden extras! In fairness to our consultant, he passed this initial test well, but then he wasn't the person we dealt with subsequently.**

The consultant will give you an overview of his services and should leave you with details of his charges, perhaps even a draft contract to mull over. Again, if he has to rush off before you have finished your questions you may be concerned he is too busy.

You are going to want to ask lots of questions at that first meeting, about him, his consultancy, his experience, his staff, his charges – and, not least, about yourself. Does he see you as landlords? Explain your situation with regard to present career, finance and family commitments, for example, and see if he can see any just cause or impediment why you should not proceed. Of course he is hoping to hook you as a client, so he is not going to paint too black a picture here, but it will be to his credit if he suggests some areas of weakness "which we can work on". Try and read between the lines of his patter and decide if he fits in with your own ethics of honesty and integrity.

Obviously, as with any contract, don't sign an agreement or hand over any money there and then. You and your partner are going to want to see more than one consultant and then make a joint and considered decision. Ask any consultants back for a second interview, or visit them, just to ensure they have the facilities and back-up resources they claim to have. New consultancies may well still be only a shell, seeking new business from hopefully gullible newcomers to finance future data bases, electronic systems and foot-soldiering research staff.

And do make sure that who you see is what you get, and what his experience in relation to your needs is. If the head of the consultancy visits you, 7-series and all, do make sure that the person handling your account is not "Oh, John Brown is joining us in a week or two from Mega Brewers, an excellent chap, known him for years." Or alternatively, "I interviewed a lad who is graduating from the local college last week, he hopes to join us after he has spent the summer in Nepal." Your problem deserves the top man, or at least a real life person with a desk and experience.

The big question might be, "has the person handling my account not only got the time to serve me properly, and the resources to back him up, but, most importantly has he any experience of actually running a pub?" After all, he is advising you how to select, buy and operate a pub, and if has not done all that himself, how can he advise you? Has he owned pubs himself, or simply worked for a brewery as, perhaps, a Business Development Manager, a job somewhat remote from the coal face task of serving beer. Again, as discussed earlier, there is a world of difference between the ethics of breweries and other businesses, and you may feel that the best consultant is one who has owned his own pub for many years and is now seeking to pass on the fruits of his wisdom rather than someone whom I would suggest has been tarred with the ethics of the brewery world.

You will want your consultant to give service in the following areas, unless you feel you are very well-versed yourself in any of them.

Rule Two – make sure the consultancy has the resources and skills in place now to give 100% of what you want in each area.

Most of these points are discussed in greater depth in the coming chapters, but in brief they are:

• *Finding a pub*

Sounds easy, but many good pubs are sold without ever coming fully onto the market, either by word of mouth, by the agent telling one or two key clients he has lined up, or by simply asking "do you want to sell?"

Anyone – it is one of your next tasks – can get themselves on estate agents' mailing lists and then copy the details received to others. What you need is inside information on what has not yet reached that stage, so you can move fast on the right pub. You can be sure that if you receive an agent's details through the post many people will have already seen the pub and crossed it off their lists of "possible" purchases. Of course, such a pub might well be right for you, but if others have rejected it, others perhaps more experienced, then it might not be quite the glittering prize you are seeking.

So, make sure your consultant has an inside track on all the latest information and has an established way of hearing about pubs coming on the market first, and that every pub he gets to hear about that even barely meets your requirements is passed on to you immediately, and without limit as to the number – it may take you several months before the right pub comes along.

• *Mystery visits and reports*

Your consultant needs to undertake on your behalf "mystery visits" to any pubs you indicate are of interest and then furnish a comprehensive written report as to the nature of that business, its likely profitability and value for money, its strengths and weaknesses, its competition, opportunities and threats. This is especially important if you are seeking pubs that are some way away from your home, if you have a full-time job which precludes you doing much visiting yourself, or if you have little business experience and need an objective appraisal.

...or visit them, just to ensure they have the facilities and back-up resources they claim to have.

Make sure your contract stipulates how many such visits and reports will be done within the agreed fee, and what the fee is for undertaking further visits and reports.

• *Price and lease negotiation*

If a third party negotiates the price of your selected pub with the vendor and his agent, this will keep you remote from such 'unpleasantries', and a strong negotiator may bring in a better deal than you would yourself, given that you want this pub and may be tempted to bid higher than common sense would suggest. But make sure your consultant is properly briefed as to what you can afford or are willing to pay as a maximum, and that he is not "splitting the difference" with the vendor: agreeing one price with you and another with the vendor and pocketing a commission at your expense. You need to firmly agree with your consultant where his limits of action are, what you yourself will do and at what stage your solicitor or accountant will take over.

• *Negotiation and liaison with the brewery*

If your pub is a leasehold one, you will need to be vetted by the brewery's local Business Development or Area Manager and your offer for the pub will be subject to the brewery's approval of you and your partner as tenants. There may also be aspects of the lease you wish to negotiate with the brewery, or more likely points they want to "negotiate" with you before they will allow you to proceed. If your consultant is a (former) landlord, experienced in the ways of breweries, it will be a great help, as against one who is a former brewery employee, who may well see things through different spectacles.

If the pub is freehold, you may need help negotiating the best discounts from your major suppliers. Not surprisingly, breweries will be falling over themselves to supply your drinks!!

• *Financial advice*

You may well need to borrow money, and your first port of call for this will be your bank. Some would say that this should be your only port of call.

Rule Three – never borrow from a brewery!!

Your consultant ought to have contacts with those specialist companies which offer financial packages for pub-buying, but be careful that there is no commitment on your part to use these services in preference to your bank – a consultant might have a business link which ties these two disparate activities closely together.

• *Business Plan*

Your consultant should prepare, with your close co-operation, a full Business Plan – you will certainly need a good one if you are borrowing money, and you need one for your own guidance as well. Pick holes in what you get – if you can see a hole your bank manager, who reads rose-tinted Business Plans every working day, will pick a hundred – and make sure your other advisers all see it and comment on it before things go to any legally-binding stage. If the figures don't stack up, throw the pub away, however sweet-smelling the roses.

• *Training*

You will need proper and professional training in a range of subjects. Does your consultant offer training which is both approved in quality and convenient in its location for you and your partner to get to? Check that the cost quoted is all-inclusive and that the end result is the full British Institute of Innkeepers Certificate.

• *Help during changeover*

Can the consultant supply a short-term and experienced relief-manager who will help you take over the pub and run it for the first week or two until you are self-supporting? Is the cost reasonable and do you like the proposed relief enough on a personal basis to get along with him in what will be very stressful days?

• *Subsequent help*

You need keeping on the straight and narrow. Will your consultant visit you at regular and agreed intervals to assess your progress, highlight where you might do better, and bring to your attention new trends or products in the market place, or even new laws, which affect your trade? Ensure the cost of these visits is detailed in the contract, and again that there is no implied requirement to use any service provided by the consultant at any time – YOU should and must be the one who decides what service is needed and when.

> **Rule Four – make sure everything is in writing before you hand over a cheque, that your solicitor is happy with the contract, and that you are fully happy with the quality and quantity of the resources available to you, and the cost of any additional follow-on services.**

> **Rule Five – the most important so far: at no stage be rushed. You might have to watch the "best pub in the world" slip out of your reach, but a rushed decision may well lead to disaster. While really good pubs are not common, another will be along, if not right behind, then fairly soon, and it may well be better still!**

• *Finally, objectivity and integrity*

Be wary of consultants who have a pub-buying, operating or refurbishment arm, for they can find themselves looking in two directions at once. If your consultant is seeking pubs for himself as well as for you, he is going to be tempted to take the best first, and if you find a good one off your own bat he might, just conceivably, try and take it off you. Before engaging a consultant, make sure his aims are yours, and that if he is also seeking to buy pubs himself his specification does not clash with yours.

• *Recommendation*

While you might need to go elsewhere for training, the best consultant is going to be a former and well-experienced landlord who has no aspirations to anything else but to find you, his number one client, the ideal pub.

You will, no doubt, seek advice, help or support from a variety of sources, but one in particular can be invaluable, and this one is not human! Start taking a regular licensed trade newspaper. We took *The Publican*, and that is one name I am happy to mention. In it you will find news and views of the industry, so you can start building up an appreciation of the issues involved, legal tips and reader's queries, and a host of advertisements and advertising supplements so you

Do you like the proposed relief enough on a personal basis to get along with him in what will be very stressful days?

can see where to get which bit of new kit, anything from glasses to cookers to large screen TVs.

Most importantly at this stage, though, *The Publican* carries a large section of advertisements of public houses for sale and of jobs in the industry. You can then start seeing just what pubs are on the market and where, and the wide range of prices, from as little as £10,000 for a city centre pub in need of a firm and experienced hand, to half a million or more for prime location pub restaurants, clubs or hotels. These advertisements will also give you a clue as to which estate agents specialise in licensed premises, and tackling this aspect is your next step.

When first considering our "Pub One" we also sought advice – local gossip might be a better description – from the local Licensed Victuallers' Association. The chairman of the branch, a landlady in fact, was most helpful and really said enough to put us off that particular pub for ever. But, as was sadly too often the case, we did not take the advice to heart....

• *Footnote on Finance*

In the final stages of writing this book, one of our very favourite pubs has just come on the market. It is situated in a small Pennine town, tucked away off the main street, a positive haven from the bustle and noise. Freehold, the asking price is a cool half million British Pounds Sterling.

Now, if you have that sort of money, and might be interested in such an outlet, consider the following alternatives.

Either you can buy the pub, work in it yourself all hours of the day, every day of the year, and perhaps make £80,000 profit per year if you are lucky (I have not seen any details of the pub so I have no specific knowledge of its financial situation.) As you will have little time to spend this kind of money, it will happily accumulate a nice nest egg for your retirement, if you survive that long running what must be a very hectic and thriving business.

Or, you can buy the pub, put in a management team and do little more than the backroom work, the accounts, the ordering, the "hiring and firing" of staff, and the publicity, for example, and leave all front of house work to others. That might leave you with £40,000 income, and essentially a 9-5 task. Not a very high return on your hard-earned capital or lucky windfall, and not a very challenging job, but at least, on the face of it, a steady living, and no commuting.

Or, you can buy a modest house in your favourite part of the world, invest the bulk of your half million and sit back and take up water colour painting, golf or sailing. And have the time, and the health, to build up any little business you might feel able to do as time passes by.

If you have half a million, is a pub the right thing to spend it on? It might well be the route for you, but consider all the angles.

Scene Three:

STARTING THE SEARCH

Re-capping on what we have established, you now have a team of advisers around you, hand-picked to fit in with your own ethos, and checked for their ability to give the type of service you want at the type of price you can afford. And you have checked that, where you have written contracts with any of these, those involved have the resources to provide the service and there are no hidden extras or commitments.

In talking with these people you will have revisited your own commitment to become a landlord, and may or may not have been shaken off that course. Relations and close friends will probably have remained fairly quiet about your plan, but there will be whispers in the background about your possible mental state!! If you know your solicitor and accountant personally they will have been cautious in their approach, a caution your enthusiasm might have over-ridden. Any advisers not personally known to you may well be urging you on, as they can see a nice fee coming their way whether you succeed or fail. You will have weighed all these aspects in the balance and pondered them in your heart, as will your partner.

You are now ready to start searching for The Pub, and the next tool you need in this task is the estate agent.

· ·

Contacting estate agents

Just as there are High Street estate agents specialising only in domestic housing, and there are others who handle mainly offices or industrial premises, so there are agents who specialise in the licensed trade. I am not sure why this should be so – we saw nothing in the five agents we dealt with most closely which suggested any talent or qualification peculiar to the licensed trade – but that is the way it is.

Like residential estate agents, licensed trade agents are a mixed bunch. Of "our five" one did things which if they are not illegal certainly ought to be, while another was protected from phone calls by two obstructive secretaries, and when he was contactable it was always on his mobile phone. Apart from disliking having to pay the high price of such calls, when we did speak it was always when he was either doing 80mph on the motorway or in another business meeting, and he made it quite clear that talking to us and selling his client's pub was not a high item on his daily agenda. Like many people, estate agents who work in prestigious offices surrounded by rich trappings and nail-varnishing secretaries may well get a false impression of their own self-importance and pass this snobbish attitude on to prospective buyers. They know they are going to sell that tedious little leasehold pub some time and collect their fat commission, so why bother trying when there is that large office block to sell, with far larger commissions, lunches and prestige?

Of the other three agents, two were fine and one was very good indeed, a professional who clearly knew his job and had everything at his finger tips. So, as with all things, there is a mixture, and if you are used to the vagaries of buying and selling a private house, you will meet the same mix of professionalism, indifference and skulduggery in buying a public one. Make a note for the future, when it comes to selling your pub – was the agent you spoke to with regard to the purchase worth doing business with?

You should register your requirements with all the agents handling pubs in your selected area. You will find their names in *The Publican* and *Dalton's Weekly*, and the local evening or weekly paper are also good sources. Be very careful how you brief them or you may miss out on the perfect place: for example agents with more than one office do not generally pass your details around the whole chain, so you will need to address each office in your selected area. Also remember that your requirements are not being handled, at this stage, by a professional agent, but by a "Job Creation" type person aided, perhaps, by a computer. If, for example, you say your top price limit is £250,000, the computer will not send you anything with an asking price of £265,000, even though something under £250,000 would be an acceptable bid. If (to be silly for the sake of illustration) you say you only want a pub with pink walls the "Job Creation" person will not have a box of this category to check before feeding the computer, so you will get all pubs, regardless of wall colour, that fit your other criteria.

Some agents will send you details of pubs that are miles outside your required area, just in case; others will contact you only rarely and you might need to phone them frequently to make sure they know you are serious – as noted above, some larger agents are so self-important and tied up dealing with large city-centre developments they put no effort into small clients like landlords, despite their claims to the contrary. Some agents send out details which are many pages long, with lots of rather irrelevant information, others confine themselves to one side of A4: some include photos, others not. The standards vary widely and you will soon realise who gives the best service, and those are the ones to bear in mind for when you come to sell.

Contrary to what it says in a book we read at this stage, details will not come flooding through your letterbox the moment you advise the agents of your requirements. As also mentioned before, quite a lot of pubs are sold without details ever having been circulated, and some agents will ignore your requests because that's the way they operate. Keep a close eye on the advertisements in papers like *The Publican* – you will regularly find pubs there which meet your criteria being sold by agents who know about you but the details of which you do not have. You will also come to recognise pubs that have been on the market for many months – a sign there is something wrong perhaps, but not necessarily something you could not handle.

Handy Tip Ten

While you will have a plan as to how long you aim to remain a landlord, plans do change, and one day sooner or later, you will want to sell. You may want to sell in a hurry – perhaps the idea has not worked out, or perhaps you or your partner have fallen ill and you can no longer cope with running the pub. If a pub has been on the market for a long time when you come to buy it, it could well take a long time to sell, unless you are aware of and can rectify any problem. A pub which has three or four people genuinely chasing it may command top price, but it will probably be easy to sell when you are ready.

So, agents' details will start arriving and you will soon start seeing pubs you want to get interested in. Your consultant should also be feeding you with details of pubs he has heard about through his network. And there is a third way to find the right place – make your own database and contact each pub on it!

For example, the whole of the UK's *Yellow Pages* are on the Internet, or indeed the paper version will be in your local library, and it is easy, if rather tedious, to make a list of all pubs in your selected area and write to the landlord of each saying words to the effect: "We are looking for a pub which meets the following criteria. We have taken your name from the *Yellow Pages*, so sorry if your pub doesn't meet our needs, but if it does and if you are thinking of selling we might be interested, let us know." OK, there is only a small chance you might get a "yes" reply, but if a landlord is looking to sell and can hook a buyer this way he will save both time and an agent's (considerable) fee, so your letter may well prompt someone who is thinking of selling to at least test the water. Neither party needs the services of an agent, and if you strike it lucky with your own mailshot it will benefit everyone.

Look carefully at each set of details received and decide if it is a "possible", and if not why not – careful analysis of pubs which become "probables" will be vital, and you need to practise your analysis techniques from Day One. Location is the most important criterium, and that means its actual geographic position, whether it fits your personal needs and what the local area is like in terms of potential and competition, but there are lots more criteria as well as those.

Mystery visits

Now comes the hard part. This is something you have to do when buying a pub, but it's also something you can do with no other business type (except allied businesses such as restaurants), let alone a domestic house search, so it can be very illuminating, and you will soon become expert as to what to look out for and what really suits you and what features put you off. I know this is a tough assignment, but someone has to do it, and now you are well established in your endeavour, you and your partner have to visit different pubs....

Read each agent's sheet you receive carefully to see if it suits you in principle. Is the domestic accommodation acceptable, is it in the right geographic location, is the price within your band, and if it is leasehold has the lease at least ten years to run? Using a detailed map, check there is nothing obviously wrong with the precise location, for example that the words "sewage works" or "airfield" are not close by the pub symbol, if those are the sort of things you would not want to be living near.

Then go and visit the pub, but tell no-one!

Your first visit can be at any time to suit you, and go in just as if you were an ordinary customer. There are 1001 things to check. Is it as advertised? It ought to be for it is illegal for the agent's details to be other than truthful, although, of course, things can be omitted or presented in their best light. As you drive towards the pub check for unwanted things in the immediate vicinity such as an incinerator or pig farm, which were not marked on the map. Stroll around the immediate neighbourhood – is there a factory or office block that is going to provide steady custom, and does it appear to be thriving or near-derelict? Perhaps it is near a railway station that is going to offer the prospect of daily commuters, or there is a new housing estate being started in the next field. Keep your eyes open for all tell-tale signs that might affect your purchasing decision. Maybe even things like a church clock which chimes all night, or a nesting flock of squawking seagulls could deter you.

Are the car park and beer garden smart, the external signs attractive and the paintwork and flowers fresh? (If it is a leasehold pub the exterior will have to be repainted every few years, so it should always be smart. If it is freehold and shabby, that is a sign that profits are not being used to further the business, if there are indeed any profits being made.)

Enter the pub. Is there a welcoming sign, fire or personal greeting? Are the staff keen to serve? Is the menu immediately available or hidden behind the bar or "sorry, we don't do food on Tuesdays". Any sign of the landlord's children playing, or of the sort of customers you might not want to attract? And already at this stage you can start building up ideas as to what you would do different so as to (hopefully) improve trade. Remember, the landlord is very keen to sell, and knows all too well that possible purchasers will be making mystery visits, so he may well suspect you, as a total stranger, of being a "possible" and react accordingly.

Order your usual drinks. Is the beer served right? If not there might be problems with the cellar – they should be easily rectifiable, but maybe many customers have taken their custom elsewhere as a result. Re-building lost trade is very hard. Take a seat and soak up the atmosphere. Without drawing attention to yourselves take notes on the whole ambiance, the numbers of customers, the proportion who have food, whether there are any signs that local clubs or groups use the bar (for example trophies or photos on the wall of "Village Soccer team 1997/98, sponsored by The Bull"): these will bring in good regular trade unless and until The Old Mill across the road offers them a better deal. Does the amount of business being done equate to the declared turnover?

Spend at least an hour doing this, then have a final discreet look around outside, move the car somewhere where you can talk without giving your little game away and compare notes with your partner. I would guess that for every ten agent's details you receive, you will visit two or three and only one will still be "in the possibles list" after this stage.

If a particular pub does stay in the "possibles pile" after this first visit, do another visit at a time when you would expect an entirely different pattern of trade. That is, if your first visit was early of a weekday evening, try going in just before last orders of a Saturday night, or on a wet Monday lunchtime, or better still both, and make

As you drive towards the pub check for unwanted things

sure there is nothing apparent which makes you cross this pub off the list.

Whether it stays on the list or not, make some written notes and keep the agent's details for future reference. For example, the price might be reduced some time in the future, or you may hear of new homes being planned nearby or of the pig farm closing, any of which may, or may not, make the pub more attractive.

If it does look good, however, now is the time to arrange a formal visit through the agent.

Formal visits

These are traditionally done mid-morning, before the staff start arriving and will take you at least an hour. (Landlords seem to be almost paranoid about the staff finding out, in case they all decide to up and leave at the faintest prospect of a new boss, although the possible sale will almost certainly be the talk of the village or community weeks before the landlord has even made up his mind to sell. I would have thought the earlier staff are told of the plans the better, so they can be kept onside, so to speak, and involved with the sale as much as is possible. Certainly they have to be told as soon as an offer is made, so perhaps it is better to discuss it with them early and break the news gently?)

Any agent worth his salt will meet you as you arrive and introduce you to the landlord and landlady, and then show you round, giving you, of course, the best possible appreciation of all the good points of his charge. As you have done at least two mystery visits you will have a great many questions, and the agent should have come prepared with, for example, draft accounts, the salient points of the lease, information on planning permissions or refusals which might affect you and other items of information concerning both the pub and the locality. And of course you will want to hear the landlord's answers to your questions: be wary of an agent who seems to be protecting his client from questions, and also be wary of an agent who does not accompany your visit but leaves the landlord to take charge. The landlord may well be more frank than an agent would be, but equally he might not be able to handle many of your more detailed questions about the lease or the locality.

If you are still interested ask to see the accounts. The ease with which these are provided is a very good indicator as to the strength of the business, and here you might find yourself in a quandary, as I shall discuss a little later. You cannot sensibly buy any business without certified accounts going back at least three years, but, because as a genre landlords prefer doing "beer things" rather than "business things" – by which I mean serving and chatting and ordering take precedence over doing accounts and carrying out marketing plans – some pubs do not have proper accounts. So be very wary of accounts which are no more up-to-date than just before the last rent review. You very much need to know the present level of profitability with the present level of rent. A good landlord will not only have bang up-to-date certified accounts ready for you, but also quarterly management accounts which will show trade up to the end of the last quarter and will be a good indicator of the business's seasonality.

Your accountant should be given a copy of all accounting information available immediately, and you should agree with him how soon and in what format he is going to let you know his views of them. You ought to be able to make a sensible assessment of them yourself, so you will have a good idea if this particular pub is still a "possible". (If you do not have previous business experience you are going to want to keep very good accounts of your pub's business yourself for the very reason that eventually you are going to want to impress a prospective purchaser, so by this stage you ought to have learned how to prepare and read accounts yourself.) If it is, do not be shy in asking for a second formal viewing if you have questions or want to check any point again. As with buying a home, go back again and again until you are happy.

Of course, the agent will be pushing you to make a decision. He is bound to tell you, unless he is unusually frank and open, that there are "several interested parties, some are ahead of you and one is a pub-operating chain with ready cash".

Handy Tip Eleven

NEVER be rushed. If someone else beats you to it, it does not matter, but it matters a great deal if you are rushed into a decision and then regret it.

Consider every aspect of the pub. If it is the one for you, in conjunction with your accountant you can make a bid.

Oh no you can't – there's lots more to do first!

SCENE FOUR:

ANALYSING PROMISING PUBS

This is where things start getting really busy, and you will almost certainly need to take time off work and travel regularly to visit pubs and have meetings, whether at home or 'away' with your various advisers. You need to progress any pubs you are interested in until that interest is terminated by finding out something which so demands. You should keep on mystery visiting new pubs as the details arrive, and you will be keeping a careful eye on your existing job and domestic commitments so things there do not start falling into controlled chaos.

So there are a number of tasks to do in parallel, and sadly, even if I could design this book in some sort of parallel format, most of its readers will not have parallel brains, so one task at a time will be related, even though you are doing five or six at once!!

You will have discussed with your consultants at an early stage their involvement in preparing reports for you, and you must be sure they have the resources to respond rapidly and professionally to your requests in this area. Once you have mystery-visited a pub and decided it is worthwhile you making a formal visit, an Outlet Assessment should be started by the consultancy, taking perhaps ten days to a fortnight to complete, so that it is ready as soon as you have made the formal viewing and are ready to consider all the pros and cons in detail.

The Outlet Assessment (OA) will vary in style, content and format from consultancy to consultancy, and it will also vary according to what you, as a client, want covering. If the pub is a long way from your present home you may need a lot more information on its locality and local services, for example, than you would if it is close at hand. And, by the by, it goes without saying that you need to ascertain with your consultant at the outset that he can properly report on pubs in the relevant area(s).

A typical OA might run to 20 pages or more. It should contain a brief and above all objective view of the pub as it presently stands, whether it is freehold or leasehold and, for example, comments on the present state of the lease and the reason why the landlord is selling, which the consultant should be able to verify independently of the selling agent.

The consultant should also visit all of the competing outlets (at this stage the word 'pub' becomes 'outlet' which is much more consultant-like!) and note in the OA the degree of competition offered, and the typical prices for standard products at these outlets compared to "your" pub. The report might well cover the strengths and weaknesses, especially in relation to these competitors or the way the pub is presently being operated, and it should also discuss in some depth the sort of people who might visit this pub compared with the others – the local demographics and whether and to how much trade depends on these folk or the "drive to" market – and thus derive a likely figure for the potential turnover and profit if the pub is run as well as it ought to be. It may or may not be presently running to its full potential, but the consultant should be able to identify ways of improving trade with you at the helm, and with him in close tandem.

All this data should be brought together, and the profitability assessed, showing whether you can firstly afford to run it with any borrowings you might need to make, and then what sort of a living it will offer you, supposing something like the optimum turnover and profitability can be rapidly achieved.

A chill will run down your spine when you first see a projected trading and profit statement and realise just how fragile the profit on even the most attractive-looking pub is!!

In essence, then, the OA should be compiled and presented in such a way and in such a timescale that it gives you the confidence to either move rapidly ahead with the particular pub, or withdraw. It should leave very few, if any, questions unanswered as to the pub's viability given your personal circumstances.

You may, of course, be interested in more than one pub at any one time, and you should have defined with the consultant how many OAs he is prepared to do and for what fee. "Good" pubs, that is ones that will suit you well and that can offer a sensible income potential, will be few and far between, and to put our own searches into this context, in the six months we were seriously looking (that is after our first attempt fell down so dramatically) we received perhaps

150 pub details from estate agent's, of which we mystery-visited 20-30. Of these we got seriously interested, to the point where we made formal visits, in just four, and we had three OAs written for us. Our search area covered a wide swathe of northern England, from Preston to York and beyond, and about 30 miles from north to south.

The bank

This is where you really need to speak with a bank manager in a branch close to the pub under scrutiny to see if he has any knowledge of it. You should also talk with your usual bank manager about the funding you might need, and what sort of paperwork he is going to want completing before he will commit to making the loan. The major banks all have a branch in every High Street, but each branch is largely autonomous when it comes to lending – do make sure both managers know what you are doing and agree the correct form of approach – if you don't tell them the truth, it is all on their desktop computers!!

This is indeed a tightrope, for if you move your bank to the selected area too soon, there is the possibility, as would have happened to us had we bought "Pub Five", of you finishing up with a bank in one town in one direction from your home, but the pub you eventually end up buying some distance in a totally different direction. While a particular banking company will have a standard policy as to what it might lend and how and when, philosophies do vary among managers, and if you talk to more than one from the same bank you may well get confused.

But, while it is good policy to keep your bank informed frequently of your progress and any changes of plan as things develop, once you have made a formal visit and had an OA prepared that looks good, you do need to see a bank manager face-to-face before you commit to something that that manager may well not feel able to support you on come the crunch!

The solicitor

If you have the good fortune to have found a good solicitor in the town in which the pub is, then he may well be a source of excellent local information, and his local publican may well know your vendor personally and of his (alleged) circumstances (through the local

You should keep on mystery visiting new pubs as the details arrive.

grapevine, of course – if your vendor uses the same solicitor as you then you have a problem and will have to find another to avoid an obvious conflict of interest arising later). In any case you ought to discuss your plans with your solicitor at this stage and should have obtained for his comment at least a "heads of agreement" digest of the lease (if it is a leasehold pub and especially if it is not a standard lease from one of the big breweries or national chains), if not the full lease, and any other documents that are readily available and which will form part of the sale. He should know what can be readily obtained at this preliminary stage and what needs leaving until after your bid has been accepted.

The accountant

Again, you need to keep this most important adviser fully informed. He may well have publicans as clients, and if so, will be able to run the rule over the figures in the OA and comment on their validity. Like the solicitor and bank manager, even if the accountant is not local to the particular pub, he should have a lot of accumulated knowledge and wisdom to inject at this stage.

Handy Tip Twelve

Take these professionals' (bank manager, solicitor and accountant) advice and do not be tempted by the view of plain wilted flowers through rose-tinted spectacles. Together your advisers should be able to put you on the right course, as they have no vested interest in seeing you into a pub, unlike the consultant who, to a certain degree, does.

Your home and job

Of course, right back on Day One you will have decided what you were going to do with your present job, or jobs plural if your partner is also in work, your present home and, if you have small children and are still determined to run a pub, what to do about child care and education. But now you are approaching crunch time in this respect, for if the OA is satisfactory and the advisers are not being too cautious, you could be putting in an offer in about two weeks' time and moving in six weeks after that.

On the other hand, it might yet be months before you have an offer accepted, it might take months for your house to sell and you may suddenly, for example, have to travel overseas on business for a month or two, a trip you might have to decline going on, and risk having to resign now anyway, as you certainly need to be in full control of "Operation Pub Find" from now on.

It is a very tricky balancing act and one which will need all your combined concentration and devotion to duty!!

Let us take a pause for breath at this stage. You may have to go through the iterative cycle of "read agent's details, mystery visit, Outlet Assessment, formal visit, consult advisers" several times before you move forward to the next square on the playing board. As you move up the ladders – and down the snakes – the accountant becomes a vital part of your thought process, so in the *Intermission* which follows I look at pubs and money, and more especially the very tight profit margins which I have already mentioned more than once.

After that I will return to the hunt, and will cover making the bid and through to moving in.

End of Part Two
Ten-Point Check List

Another chance to pause and reflect, and, again, before proceeding, you should have safely passed all these Check Points:

1 Have you established the right team of advisers to give you the advice you are going to need, and have you checked that these advisers have the resources in place now to provide that advice when required and at a pre-agreed price?

2 Have you registered your interests with all relevant estate agents, and have you checked you are getting information from them which is timely and relevant?

3 Have you discussed your plan with your bank manager, and assured yourself that you have the necessary funds available to do what you want?

4 Have you arranged to have the right sort of training? I'll cover this subject in depth after the Intermission. And booked time off work, etc., where appropriate?

5 Are you finding, when doing your mystery visits, that the right sort of pubs for you are coming on the market at the right sort of price?

6 Is your enthusiasm for this plan still as high as ever?

7 Are you getting quality and speedy Outlet Assessments from your consultant, and are the figures therein holding up to your expectations?

8 Have you made plans to sell your house, resign from your job(s), change the children's school, and all the other domestic things that need to be tied in with the upheaval that is about to start?

9 Revisit all of this book, especially the Check List at the end of Part One.

10 Are you still really sure? Read the following Intermission and check, check, check!!

Intermission

PUBS AND MONEY, OR LACK OF IT

A review of the financial aspects of running a pub, whether leasehold or freehold.

Question time. Three men come into your pub and order three pints of bitter. And they have another round, and then a third before departing. Nothing unusual, you will be hoping for many such events every week. So they bought nine pints altogether, at, say, £1.40 a pint, total £12.60.

So, how much of that is for you personally to spend as part of your domestic budget and how much goes into the running of the pub and taxes? £5, £3, £1.50? In this Intermission I will take you through some of the financial implications of being a landlord.

Firstly, a key parameter by which your business profitability will be measured is Gross Profit Percentage (GP%), which is defined as

$$\text{Gross Profit Percentage} = \frac{\text{(Selling price minus cost of item)}}{\text{selling price}} \times 100$$

(all figures net of VAT)

While this is not a book of facts to learn, this one is so basic that it should be tattooed on your forehead now!!

Now, to survive, this figure needs to be, if at all possible, over 50%, or in other words if you buy an item in at £1, net of VAT, you should sell it for at least £2 net of VAT. This is the sort of mark-up that causes apoplectic convulsions among the staff of consumer watchdog-type TV and radio programmes who have no idea about business, but do know that anyone marking up goods at all should be publicly hanged for extortion. But if you do not achieve an overall GP% of 50%+ you will be in trouble, and if it declines, things will get worse. Your first target when you move in is to hit 50% overall, and then try and improve it, without losing turnover because people feel you are too expensive and start going to your competitors.

Earlier on I mentioned that the brewery would sell you a 36-gallon barrel of bitter beer for around £220 net of VAT (north of England 1998 prices). The price varies according to the strength of the beer, and not unnaturally(??) it is more expensive when bought in those parts of the country the breweries feel will stand a higher price than others.

£220 for 36 gallons equals 76.5p a pint. To get a 50% GP% you must double this, that is 153p, and then add VAT before selling, making the final selling price 180p. Not many (northern) locations can stand a price of 180p for a pint of decent bitter, and remember, to achieve your GP% target you need to sell all the beer in your barrels: the barrels delivered will be at the most 18 gallons, and there will always be wastage and spillage, not to mention free drinks, legitimate or otherwise.

Fortunately for your financial sanity, your GP% target is an overall figure, including all drinks and all food. In a tied leasehold pub, where there's no discount on the beer you buy as part of the "tie", your drinks GP%, aided by the higher mark-ups on soft drinks (buy for under 10p a half pint, sell for at east 50p, often much more) and by the discounts you can negotiate on your "guest" beer (remember, £60 a barrel equals a 21p a pint discount, net of VAT) and on other non-tied products including spirits, will be about 45%. In a free house you ought to be able to get over 50% on wet sales, and both types of pub should make a GP% of 55% on all food (dry sales) which is one reason for the growth in food sales in even the most humble local pub.

It is an irony of the debate over drink-driving that many landlords see the possibility of a lower limit, being discussed as this book is being written, meaning that drivers will visit pubs less as they will be

But do know that anyone marking up goods at all should be publicly hanged for extortion.

able to drink less beer or spirits without exceeding the proposed limit. But if drivers switch to soft drinks, as they usually do, the profit for the landlord is actually far higher, pint for pint, so the more customers who drink halves of lemonade or cola, the higher the profit. Most landlords would do best selling no beer, especially tied beer, at all! (But, serious point, beware of "shortfall charges," whereby the brewery penalises you if you fail to reach its stipulated target for beer sales.)

It is essential your GP% is as high as the market will take, but it depends not just on the prices you can charge – your competitors will largely decide that – but also on the discounts you can negotiate with your suppliers and, more importantly, your control over wastage, spillage and "give and take away-age." On the food side, portion control is king, and meals should be served with just enough food on the plate to satisfy the diner. How often do you go into a pub and order a meal, only to be faced with a huge portion, the landlord somehow believing that giving you vast amounts of chips you are never going to eat is somehow a good thing. Apart from probably putting you off the place for ever, every chip that you don't eat and send back is waste food and waste profit, food which could have been served to the next person and the proper profit achieved. But I digress – food service is well outside the scope of this book!

Let us now look at some typical figures and see how much profit there is at the end of the day.

First of all, take a typical leasehold pub doing good all-day business in an affluent area. Let us suppose it has a turnover, including VAT, of £350,000. That is pretty high, especially for the sort of pub you, as a newcomer to the business, might aspire to, so it is "top of the range". If one were to be sold with a good part of the lease remaining and no evident drawbacks, the leasehold ought to sell for around £100,000.

So, turnover £350,000 including VAT, equals in round figures, £298,000 net of VAT, and all future figures are net of VAT. Two immediate things are evident: every week you have to put £1000 aside for the VAT man, who does not knock twice, and a £350,000 gross turnover roughly means that on a good Saturday night you will take £1000 in the till. So you are working all Saturday night for HM Customs and Excise!!

Now, out of the £298,000 net takings you are looking for an overall GP% of 50%. You need to concentrate heavily on food, and to make the sums simple we will assume you take just as much on food as on drinks – known in the trade as a 50:50 wet:dry split. Because the profit is more on food you want to try and sell more, but as I say, we are keeping the sums simple. And if we say the GP% is 45 on drinks and 55 on food, that will give us an overall figure of 50%, in other words out of the £298,000 takings, £149,000 goes on buying stock, leaving £149,000.

Riches indeed. £150,000 a year, marvellous!, Err, not quite. One or two other people want a slice of the pie before you can go out and buy even a jar of coffee, let alone that holiday in the Algarve.

Let us look first at the fixed costs, those costs you have to pay even if you never open your doors. First and foremost is the brewery rent, which, as I have related, will go incessantly up, will go up all the more if you do good business and the brewery will get very heavy very rapidly if you are late in paying.

Handy Tip Thirteen – Bonds

The brewery will demand a bond, usually equal to one quarter's rent or one month's beer supplies, but often more, before it will allow you to take over a lease. It does this on the assumption that you are dishonest by nature and are bound to do a runner owing it rent or money for beer. In other words the brewery gets its rent a quarter in advance (it may demand it is paid monthly just to be even safer), and then it wants another quarter's before you move in to guard against this assumed dishonesty (or looked at the other way, you are paying for your first beer orders before you actually order them and are always one month ahead). You need to build this figure – allow at least £10,000 – into your financial equations when considering if you can afford a certain pub. Sometime bonds are made by depositing the demanded figure in a building society account for which the brewery holds the pass book, only giving you it back if you leave the pub in a proper fashion with no dues. Or it may simply demand a higher rent. In the last pub we looked at we assumed the bond would be wanted in passbook form, so we duly deposited the money, only for the brewery to demand 25% extra rent, a sum which we simply could not afford to pay out of the pub's takings.

The tip is to be aware of this bond and sort it out with the brewery at a very early stage, and, to preclude any misunderstanding, get the requirement on paper, signed by a senior manager.

OK, a typical rent is £33,000 a year, usually paid quarterly by direct debit. And just to remind you it will be reviewed upwards in the light of the business the brewery thinks you should be doing every three or five years (the dates will be in the lease). You are expected to try and negotiate this rise down and a little leeway might be given but not enough to offset your costs of the negotiation, and it is quite usual for the rent to actually rise each year. £33,000 immediately after the review, £34,500 the following 12 months, £36,000 the next 12 months and then a statutory review, and expect a demand for at least £40,000. Make sure these rises are built into your projections.

£149,000 less £33,000 equals £116,000.

Then the council will want the business rate – expect a typical £7500 (and remember, you still have domestic Council Tax to pay on your living accommodation), and then perhaps £500 for emptying the dustbins – yes, that's an extra charge for commercial premises, and you will pay extra the more bins you have to empty. And while not actually fixed, you might expect gas, water and electric to total £12,000 in a full year: And £2500 for insurance. This batch totals £15,000, leaving you with £101,000 – just £4.05 out of the £12.60 spent by the three men at the beginning of this episode.

But it doesn't stop there. A small item is repairs. The lease will almost certainly be a "fully repairing" one, meaning you have to do all repairs as if you owned the freehold, and there will be a stiff clause in the lease demanding you decorate the pub inside and out, usually in the colours approved by the brewery, every few years – the period will be stipulated and you will be checked for new paint!! You will also use the phone to make orders, etc., buy materials for cleaning, have a window cleaner, make car trips to the cash and carry, etc., and all sorts of similar sundry payments – allow £14,000 for these over a year, reducing your balance to £87,000.

Then comes the biggest slice of the cake, staff wages. Even if you and your partner work for free behind the bar most days, you will still need a pool of several bar staff and a cleaner, as well as a chef and at least one assistant. Decent chefs are scarce and cost decent wages, and you will need cover lunchtimes and evenings seven days a week, 365 days a year. Staff costs, including national insurance, could be around £60,000 in a full year. That might sound a huge sum, but you will be open for trading around 4500 hours a year. Two bar staff and two in the kitchen at all times will easily eat up that sum.

And when calculating staff costs, don't rely on the out-going landlord's figures or rates. Decide how many man-hours you are going to need and the wages you are prepared to pay and calculate your profitability accordingly. Remember that if you pay peanuts you will get monkeys, so if you want smart and conscientious staff pay them well. Marks & Spencer doesn't have really good staff because they all like working there – the company pays above-industry-average wages to get the right people for the kind of service they are dedicated to providing. You will have to do the same, if you want to offer good service.

And do take account of any likely future minimum wage regulations. As I write these words the government is said to be considering £3.60 an hour as the adult minimum wage: that is quite a bit more than many bar staff get, and while I personally welcome such a move it will have a major effect on pub profitability, slim enough as it is already.

So after deducting these hypothetical staff costs, that leaves you with just £27,000. Hardly a fat salary, and while some of those costs may be a bit on the high side, they are not wildly so and are based on actual experience. And you still have to pay for marketing: advertisements, production of menus and signboards, perhaps a newspaper or newsletter to circulate in the locality. Marketing is the item most usually totally under-funded in a pub, but as you have only £27,000 left you will be tempted to save in this area, as it is about the only option you have. But if you do not market the pub how are people going to know you are there?

And finally you have to pay for new or hired kit and equipment, everything from glasses to freezers and cookers, fees for your solicitor,

Remember that if you pay peanuts you will get monkeys.

accountant and consultant. And oh, don't forget the bank loan repayments and bank charges.

Conservatively, the net profit available to you on this kind of pub, even if it is run well and to its full potential, before you take any money out for yourselves whatsoever, is typically 8% of net turnover, that is £24,000 from a £300,000 net, £350,000 gross of VAT operation. Of the £12.60 the three men spent, you get to keep less than £1.

And then you have to pay your own tax and national insurance, council tax, etc., etc....

So, in other words, you are running a highly successful pub, working, both of you, 80-100 hours a week and making perhaps, if you do well, £500 a week between you, gross of tax. Or about £3 an hour.

And remember, that is running a pub to its maximum potential. You are newcomers and have to learn the ropes, so you will certainly not hit 100% potential even in the first year. Let us quickly look at some effects of trading below top notch.

Firstly, though, let's summarise the above figures so we can see how changes might affect the bottom line.

Turnover		£350,000
Less VAT at 17.5%	£52,000	£298,000
Cost of stock purchases at 50% overall GP%	£149,000	£149,000
Typical rent	£33,000	£116,000
Business rates and utilities	£15,000	£101,000
Repairs, redecoration, phone, travel, sundries	£14,000	£87,000
Staff costs	£60,000	£27,000

Not included: marketing (allow at least £5000 a year, especially at the start), consultancy and professional fees (£3000+), and the hire and purchase of kit and equipment (depends what is already there, how new it is and what you need to replace or introduce).

So, suppose you find you do not make the £350,000 projected turnover: a local factory closes, your face doesn't quite fit and some regulars leave, the local competition gets a new, fully-trained and very keen manager who improves value enormously, or the weather is bad and tourists don't arrive in their usual numbers.

A simple 10% reduction in trade, something you will hardly notice if you are only counting bums on seats and not watching every day's takings like a hawk, will bring turnover down to £315,000 gross, £268,000 after VAT, or £134,000 after purchasing stock. But all the other items, the four between the dashed lines in the above summary, remain the same unless and until you can respond with added marketing or whatever, and total £122,000 – the £27,000 "profit" has shrunk to £12,000 and you need to spend more on marketing to see more trade. That's perilously close to a trading loss.

Or, suppose the staff see you as a gullible newcomer and start fiddling you, just a bit. Or chef isn't very good at stock control. Or the beer cooler breaks down and you lose a few barrels. Or you like a pint or two yourself each evening and take it out of the bar stock without paying for it (the VAT men will still want the VAT on this "free" beer!!). Suppose your overall GP% drops to 45%, as it easily can if you are not very sharp.

Assuming your turnover stays the same, at £298,000 net of VAT, but your costs of stock rises to £163,000. This leaves you with £135,000 instead of £149,000 gross profit, or £13,000 at the bottom line. If trade drops by 10% and GP% by five percentage points you will be running at a loss.

I hope these illustrative figures demonstrate just how fine a line it is between profit and loss, especially in a tied leasehold pub.

Things are better in a freehold pub, but remember, lest what follows looks very lucrative, you have upwards of £250,000 tied up in the property, which could be earning you a substantial investment income, or it is costing you most of your profit by way of mortgage repayment.

Freehold profit potential

Possibly because such places are "snapped up" by the pub-owning chains for their profit potential, there do seem to be relatively few freehold pubs on the market at over £250,000. On the other hand, as a rough rule of thumb the asking price for a freehold pub is in the region of £90,000 plus the annual turnover net of VAT, and I would suggest that any pub with an asking price of under £200,000 is not going to give you a sensible income, unless you especially like the idea of a very rural pub and are not too bothered about income, preferring the peace and atmosphere instead. Thus I will take as an example a freehold pub with an asking price of £250,000, which roughly equates to a turnover, net of VAT, of £160,000.

Now of course your profitability in a freehold pub is very much better than in a leasehold one – you have no brewery tie, so can negotiate the price of your beers from whomsoever you feel will give you the best profitability, and, much more importantly, you have no lease payments to make.

Being able to buy your beers wherever you choose means you should be able to attain 55% GP% on your drinks sales, instead of 45% in a lease pub, as well as maintaining 55% on food, giving you 55% overall, rather than 50%.

The summary table above can thus be modified thus for such a typical freehold pub:

Turnover		£188,000
Less VAT at 17.5%	£28,000	£160,000
Cost of stock purchases at 55% overall GP%	£72,000	£88,000
Typical rent	£nil	£88,000
Business Rates and utilities	£11,000	£77,000
Repairs, redecoration, phone, travel, sundries	£11,000	£66,000
Staff costs	£40,000	£26,000

Freehold

Not included, as before, are marketing (allow at least £5000 a year, especially at the start), consultancy and professional fees (£3000+), and the hire and purchase of kit and equipment (depends what is already there, how new it is and what you need to replace or introduce).

I have reduced the costs of rates and utilities since this sample pub will be smaller than the leased one illustrated earlier, and similarly repairs and redecoration ought to be less, especially as there will be no legal obligation to redecorate to a fixed schedule. And thus, if staff costs are also trimmed in line with the smaller operation, you can see that – and again I do emphasise this is a rough calculation for the purposes of illustration – a £250,000 freehold pub with a net turnover of £160,00 will have the same "bottom line" as a leasehold pub costing between £70,000 and £100,000 and with a turnover twice as high.

Some of the costs noted above are truly fixed, rates and rent, for example, while others you can minimise by keeping a close eye on them, such as heat and light and telephone. Only one item is really under your full control and that is staff costs. When we were planning to own a pub, we took the view that there was enough to do behind the scenes managing a £250,000-a year business that we would only be in the bar occasionally, and that we would employ experienced bar staff to give the pub a professional image. Thus our allowance for staff costs was rather high, and our profit consequentially lower. On the other hand, some people believe that a landlord's place is behind the bar and mingling with customers as many hours of the day as possible, and if this is your philosophy you will need to "purchase" fewer staff hours. Better still, if you or your partner is a qualified chef and plans to do most of the cooking you can save a significant proportion of the staff costs suggested above, with subsequent increase in the bottom line profit.

But whether in practice you can achieve such GP% targets, or maintain the declared turnover of the outgoing landlord or the potential turnover suggested by your consultant's studies is another matter. For me the two big questions are:

1 Can you work happily under a brewery lease, with all its strictures?

2 If you have £250,000 to invest in a new business, is a freehold pub with a potential before tax income of less than £30,000 (and possibly far less, especially initially) the right place for such money?

In the end it boils down to personal philosophy: if you fancy a country freehold pub, preferring the lifestyle to riches and are happy to risk your quarter of a million nest egg, plus moving expenses of course, then profitability forecasts are not going to be the issue. Equally you may have no chance of raising a quarter of a million but be quite happy to lease a pub to learn the ropes for far less outlay, and then move on to bigger and better things, or move out, having lost little except sleep, after a few years.

But in a leasehold pub less than 10p in every pound that enters your till is yours, and in a freehold pub you might really watch the pennies and keep hold of 15p in the pound.

Coincidental Footnote 3

As this book was being prepared for printing, another local landlord made the headlines of the local paper. The man was found guilty at the Bury magistrates' court of showing a Sky TV football match to his customers without the appropriate licence. If you play background music in your pub you will almost certainly need two licences in order to help recompense the artists and recording companies. Whether this is right or not depends on your point of view, but if you don't have the correct licences you will doubtless be visited by someone who strongly believes the law is right. They will check for the total absence of music, and take you to court, just as if you had no TV licence, if you are in breach of the law.

If you want to show Sky TV to your customers, Sky will also charge you a not inconsiderable fee for the privilege – you can't simply take the domestic TV and set it up in the Snug whenever there is a football match on, Sky will charge you. (And it places large advertisements in *The Publican*, for one, warning those who might try to get away with not paying this charge of the dire consequences.) Before installing a TV you will, of course, check the charges, assess if and by how much they might rise in the future, and decide whether the extra custom will pay the costs.

BUT, you also need another licence to show any television programme to a public audience, e.g. your customers, and this can cost up to £200.

Now this landlord failed to buy this particular licence and showed, it was said in the paper, just one football match.

The fine was £500 plus £200 costs (plus of course his own costs), which shows just how serious magistrates take this type of law. Again, with the figures in this Intermission, you can see how many pints the landlord had to sell to pay the fine from the profit.

Do assess all charges against likely profit before committing yourself to music, a TV, a games area or live artists! And make sure all licences are properly reflected in your business plan, they are a significant item.

On the other hand, some people believe that a landlord's place is behind the bar and mingling with customers as many hours of the day as possible.

Act 3

· ·

TOWARDS CHANGEOVER DAY, CAREFULLY

The scene is set in numerous locations, mainly pubs and offices, but eventually settles down to being behind the bar of "Ye Olde Perfect Inn".

SCENE ONE:

TRAINING AND LEARNING

"Training, training, who needs training to run a pub? I've been watching the girls at the Lamb and Ferret these past five years and it's a piece of cake. You stand there, smile, pull a few pints, have a joke or two, pull a few more pints, have one for yourself and cash up at the end of the night. Dead easy, I'm not going to need training, can't afford it anyway..."

Well, of course you are going to need it, and lots of really good training as well, and you cannot afford not to. You have to for the benefit of the local magistrates, but you also have to otherwise you really will sink when you realise how little you really know. Training won't tell you everything, or give you experience, but it will get you on the ladder, safely.

· ·

What's it got to do with magistrates?

Even if you do not want to go on a training course, the magistrates, more formally known as the Licensing Justices, in front of whom you will shortly have to stand, doff your cap and act all respectful, will probably – indeed almost certainly – insist you do.

Once you have decided firmly on the administrative area in which your new pub is to be, then you should contact the Clerk to the Magistrates at the local court and ask for the guidance notes which their worshipfulnesses will have issued regarding new licensees applying for on-licences. The notes will lay down rules, which, of course, the magistrates may or may not abide by but you will only find that out as you go along, and one of these will may well be that you have the full British Institute of Innkeepers' certificate, and the Primary Certificate in Food Hygiene, before they will grant your licence application.

And to be awarded those certificates (the appearance of which in court may well surprise some of the old hands!) you need to go on an approved course of training and pass the examinations.

As an example, my home town, Bury in Greater Manchester, issues "Statement of Policy and Procedure, the Licensing Justices for the Petty Sessional Division of Bury".

The salient point therein says that "in considering the suitability of an applicant to hold any Justice's Licence, the committee regards the holding of a National Licensee's Certificate or equivalent as being a desirable attribute. Possession or otherwise of such certificates/qualification in no way alters the requirement of the committee to be satisfied in all cases that the applicant is a fit and proper person to hold a Justice's Licence." (the NLC forms a part of the full BII certificate).

It is well worth asking for the local equivalent of this document from the court or council most appropriate to your target pub or pubs so you can be fully aware of the Licensing Justices' requirements and ensure you have the required certificates, before you apply for your licence.

It is beyond the scope of this book to discuss what you will learn on your course – there are plenty of books on the subject, and the BII manuals are excellent – but here are some of the topics covered in the courses:

Bar and cellar management – and you need hands-on experience of both, not just classroom stuff.

Employment law and recruitment – a minefield these days with all the employee protection there is.

Training skills, operational standards, hygiene and health and safety – you need to be able to train your staff to meet the high standards you will insist on and to abide by all aspect of Hygiene and H&S law, another minefield for the inexperienced. Once you have your own pub you will need to pay particular attention to changes in law and regulation in this sensitive area, as well as those in employment.

Social responsibilities – The law, security and drug awareness – avoiding break-ins, thefts, drug abuse and all other aspects relating to the law (not just licensing law) and the police.

Lifestyle – running a pub is a 100+ hours a week commitment, which is going to be very different from anything you have done before, so be prepared! A few hours spent learning about stress management will pay dividends.

Financial management – absolutely crucial if you are to avoid going under, let alone prosper, especially if you have never run a business or kept accounts before.

Marketing – so often neglected but no less vital, than any other aspect.

Catering – a very different operation than serving drinks, but all under your roof.

Machines management – gaming machines can bring you much-needed added profit at very little if any direct outlay: you need to maximise this potential.

How to buy a pub (you may have already done a bit of this for real!!) and what happens on and either side of changeover day.

All in all there is a lot to learn, and you need to master every bit of it. You will have gathered from the words so far that the pace is building up as you near actually agreeing to buy a pub, so the earlier you do your training and get it out of the way and the certificates framed, the better.

While some of our consultants' actions, or lack of actions, are crticised in this book, we have to be fair and say that their training, and their main "training man", was really very good indeed. All the above subjects can be learned in sufficient detail to enable you to pass the exams in a week by some furious teaching and evening study, but it is best spread over two wccks, if you have the time and money. At the very least you should get first class course notes, and an up-date service, which should be a source of reference for years to come. But there is no substitute for experience!

At the end of the course you will sit exams for the certificates noted above. The exams are not hard, and your lecturers should have given you very broad hints as to what to expect. I have an added problem that I am "visually challenged" and cannot see to write and subsequently read notes made during sessions and had to rely on memory. Nevertheless I passed easily. Of course, your trainer or examiner might take a stiffer line than ours did. In one of the BII exams you have to get all of the first ten questions right, and then, I think, 36 right out of the next 40. When we took that exam the first ten answers were checked as soon as we had written them down, and if we had got all ten right – which everyone there did – we were allowed to go on to the second part. But the next course had a different examiner who marked all 50 questions at the end of the whole exam – some people got one of the first ten wrong and had to come back at a later date to re-sit. As in everything, some people are helpful while others cannot see past the end of the rule book.

Handy Tip Fourteen

The BII exams are fair, but the questions are very precisely written and the answers – almost always having multiple choice answers where you tick one of a number of boxes

*A few hours spent learning about stress management will
pay dividends.*

– are equally precisely put. Make sure you read the question carefully, do not jump to a conclusion that a question must mean something when careful reading will show it means something else. There are no trick or obtuse questions, but you need to take care!

You will find a lot on the course which reinforces points made in this book, as well as a great deal that will be very new to you. Again I would suggest undergoing the training as soon as you are committed on the road towards buying a pub, so that all the many things you will learn, not least from talking with others on the course who may already have pub experience, can be put to good effect as soon and as often as possible. (More and more experienced landlords are taking these training courses as, in many areas, having the BII certificate is becoming a magistrates' requirement for the renewal of a licence, not just the granting of it.)

And a small but important point: do make sure you actually get your certificates. Ours, shall we say, got "delayed" by several weeks, and in the end only some "determined effort" got them to us in time for us to show them to the magistrates at the licence transfer hearing. You might not strictly speaking need to show them, but it is certainly brownie points if you do, and if you don't have them on the day you can bet the magistrate will be in a bad mood and demand you go away and get them, for the next session in a month's time!! (And you can't take over the pub without the licence being granted.)

Other things to learn

While on the subject of learning, two other things you need to do before you move in: talk to the police and get real hands-on experience behind a bar.

The first you cannot really do until you know for sure where you are moving to, but you will find the local police most helpful and eager to know you and your plans. You need to talk to the local licensing officer, who keeps a fatherly eye on all licensed premises in the area or division, and also the sergeant or inspector in charge of the local area in which your pub actually is. They will be a good source of information regarding any problems they experience with pubs in general or particular, and more especially if your pub already has a "reputation".

The police will also give you excellent brochures, and possibly even a video, on how to detect the use or sale of illegal substances on your premises, and will eagerly advise on security matters. They will take the view very strongly that an hour spent advising you now may well save them days of leg and paperwork later, and they are as anxious not to see the inside of your pub as you will be not to see them there! If you need the police they will treat a call from a pub as a priority unless the calls become so frequent that they are a nuisance. Only call on their services when you have a real problem, but if you get real problems too often, expect an objection when you come to renew your licence.

Getting hands-on experience is a must. Your present local landlord will, or ought to be, delighted to give you this experience, and a bit of *ad hoc* training, if you'll work for no pay, and you really do need to learn how to serve all kinds of drinks, get used to prices and a till system, handle all kinds of customers, deal with any unpleasantries, and mop up vomit from the ladies' toilets!

Handy Tip Fifteen

The Scottish & Newcastle Internet website referred to earlier has a paragraph on training, in which it says "new tenants initially attend a five-day residential Core Skills Training programme. While much time is given to the practical skills of running a pub, the course places a unique focus on ensuring tenants can maximise the profit potential of running a small business. This is particularly important given the financial investment of the tenant. From there, tenants go on to benefit from a range of on-going training courses tailored to their specific needs. In addition, each tenant is assigned a tenancy business manager who will work with them to maximise profits...."

You cannot get enough training, but you may well have spent upwards of £1000 on a private training course in the early stages of your pub-hunt. If you are buying a leased pub, you need to check with the landlord's area manager in the early stages of interest what training his company will insist you have, given your specific situation, before you can take over the lease. It may be that if you

and your partner both have to attend such a five-day
residential course as noted above it may have
implications regarding your present job or child care, for
example. It may also be difficult to fit in five days away
when you are in the final stages of buying a pub, giving
up your job and selling your home, but if the brewery/
landlord says it is a condition of the sale then you will
have to comply. It may also be that the availability of
places on such a course may delay the completion of the
lease purchase. For example, a period of six weeks from
"offer acceptance" to "changeover day" is a reasonable
timespan for the legal and financial aspects of the sale,
and you may well be planning to give up work on a
certain day and then move in on another. If, two weeks
into that process you are talking with the area manager
and he says the courses are mandatory, are held monthly
at the other end of the country and that the next two
are already fully-booked, you might suddenly have a
considerable delay on your hands, during which time
you have, perhaps, no income and even no home!!

As a final note on tenancies and the S&N website, it also notes that
"in 1997 the company undertook over 100 joint refurbishments with
tenants, which for the first time included a number of new pub
brands" (such as Cooper's kitchen). "All the tenants who have been
involved in developing these new brands have been delighted with
the upturn in business they have seen as a result."

As a tenant you may not have the freedom to keep the style,
atmosphere and image of "your" pub the way you want it to be. Or
of course, you may well be genuinely delighted to be turned from an
ordinary pub to a branded one, who knows!

SCENE TWO:

GETTING THERE, MAKING A BID AND MOVING FORWARD

To recap after the diversions of the last two sections, you have been
sent loads of agents' details, paid mystery visits to several of those
pubs and become sufficiently interested in two or three for you to

You really do need to learn how to serve all kinds of drinks.

make formal visits and for your consultant to have prepared Outlet Assessments. Your bank manager is in the loop and has indicated that the necessary funding will be available, and you have taken steps to sell your present house, leave your job and change the children's schools, as appropriate to your own circumstances.

Now is the time to take a deep breath, hold your nose and take the plunge into the freezing waters – it's time to make an offer.

You immediately have a problem to resolve, before the words "X thousand pounds" pass your lips. If the pub is new on the market and is a good one there may well be quite a few other parties interested and you may need to move fairly rapidly to "win the bidding battle". On the other hand, if the pub has been on the market for six months or more you can take your time, try a low offer and really delve deep to make sure there is no hidden problem at the root of the slowness of the pub to sell. You want a good pub that will offer you and your partner the right location and the right income, but you may be able to get a very good bargain if this "slow to sell" pub has been on the market for some time, the owner is getting desperate, and whatever the problem is that has deterred others is not a problem for you and your partner.

So, you have found the pub, or certainly the best of the bunch so far, and you want to make a bid.

Handy Tip Sixteen

At this stage, whether you make a bid verbally or in writing, it is not binding (although do add the words "subject to contract" to anything you put in writing so as not to be caught out by a clever lawyer!) As with a house purchase, your offer is not binding until you have exchanged contracts, and even then people have been known to renege on deals!!

You may want to discuss your offer directly with the vendor, or with the selling estate agent, or have your consultant negotiate on your behalf. I feel happier with this last course personally, as long as the consultant has a proper brief as to your limits and desires and does not, as ours did in his enthusiasm, steam ahead on his own. It is an idea to decouple yourself from the emotions which surround such landmark events, but whichever way you choose, you will need to confirm your bid in writing to the agent and to provide evidence, such as a letter from the bank manager or a photocopy of a bank statement, that you have the financial wherewithal. And as newcomers to the trade, it is best to reassure all concerned by saying you have all the relevant certificates and know of no impediment why their worshipfulnesses should not grant the transfer of the licence.

Then, just as in house-buying, you will hear if you have been successful or not, and if you have the fun really starts. If not, do make sure the agent retains you on the "interested" pile, in case the successful bidder should fall by the wayside for some reason – which reason you will want to know – and your bid can be revived. And there is no reason why you should not have more than one bid active at any one time, as long as you can afford the time and the consultants' fees. You very well may not succeed in finally buying the "number one" pub, so you need to be riding as many horses as is sensible.

The Business Plan

Whether or not you are borrowing money you will need a good business plan, one which is objectively worked out, with the rose-tints firmly locked out of sight, and which shows the full trading picture for 18 or even 24 months ahead.

You will have started building up this plan long before you actually found the right pub, for you will have realised the likely sales income and the various expenditures of your target pub, and this one that you are bidding on won't be far removed from that base line.

The business plan should firstly describe the pub, and go on from the Outlet Assessment to discuss what you want to do with it, in terms of improving trade, marketing, signage, staff, product offering, etc., etc. (within the limits of any lease, tie or other obligation), and any capital expenditure planned should be detailed, as best you can judge, and a timescale assigned to it, e.g. before we complete, in the first year, when it can be afforded, etc.

You should then detail every known and likely expenditure, including any bank charges or interest payments, and also your target income both for food and drink, on a calendar month basis, or, if you prefer, a four-week accounting period. Don't forget to take account of VAT payments – your income through the till will include VAT, which you have to repay to HM Customs & Excise every three months. You can, at the time when you register your business for VAT, request which dates you make your VAT return on. (These Quarterly Dates are the last dates in the respective months and you have to pay the VAT due before the last day of the following month.) Your business plan should reflect the payment of, effectively, 17.5% of all income back to Customs and Excise on these due dates. Of course some of your purchases will also have been invoiced to you with VAT added, so you will have some amount to offset against your "sales VAT".

Handy Tip Seventeen

You can register your pub business for VAT as soon as you have firmly established that you are going into the pub trade, and can thus reclaim any VAT on, for example, training courses or consultants' fees. The timing needs careful consideration with your accountant and HM Customs. You can reclaim VAT on such "purchases" retrospectively, but there are limits, if you reclaim VAT on, say, a training course, and then decide not to buy a pub after all, you may have to pay the reclaimed VAT back to HM Customs.

It also certainly makes life simpler if you can arrange for the relevant VAT Quarter Date so that it coincides with your financial year end.

The business plan should take the present trading as a baseline, and then be refined to indicate the level of trading and expenditure you feel you will honestly achieve. Don't fool yourself by being optimistic: in the first few weeks you may gain a bit of trade as locals come in to see if you are as good, or bad, as Old Harry, and some will not come back when they realise you have indeed got bad breath, serve flat beer and beat the wife in public. The trade may well pick up as you do new things which attract more folk – a lot depends on how good a ship the outgoing landlord was running and whether you honestly believe you can do better. It is vital the income shown on the business plan is an honest judgement – it is your goal to meet those figures and thus achieve the required profit, but if the target is too high you will never make it and you will always be struggling on the back side of the drag curve, as they say in aeronautical circles, running to stand still.

Equally, make sure that all costs are properly assessed. Check the business rates payable with the council (and the charge for refuse collection), for example, don't take the agent's word for it.

Calculate very carefully the staff costs: you'll need to assess how many staff you will need, bearing in mind how many and which hours you and your partner plan on working behind the bar or in the kitchen. Make an allowance for emergency staff to cater for those taking holidays, being sick or simply not arriving for work. Check with the outgoing landlord the hourly rate paid to each of the present staff, and where applicable don't forget national insurance contributions.

An area we found "of interest" was telephone costs. These can be quite large if a staff member likes phoning a cousin in Nigeria every day and you don't have the strength of character to stop it. Most of the calls you make as part of the pub's business will be to suppliers within the local call area: faxing orders saves both time and errors, better still get them to call you, as the brewery most certainly will. On the other hand, a public telephone located in the trading area can bring in a steady income, and maybe even balance out the costs of your business calls – you can set the rate these phones charge, depending on whether you look on them as a source of income or as an altruistic service to inebriates needing taxis! One of "our five" pubs declared an annual "telephone plus postage" cost of under £100, and actually showed a profit in one quarter, while another had an annual phone bill of over £1900! Given that weekday local area phone calls are 3p a minute, that's an awful lot of calls! As a sideline, that pub's declared profit in that year was under £4500, a figure which could have been 50% higher if the phone bill had been more realistic, or more carefully controlled.

You should also look very carefully into the seasonality of the business, and how you might fare during the winter months. One of "our five" was located in a superb Yorkshire Dales village, with lots of local trade but also a great many tourists from Easter to October. The owner kept truly excellent accounts, split into trading quarters, and these showed that in the winter months the pub actually traded at a loss, and only made profits when the tourists arrived. Bearing in mind that the pub will have been packed in the Christmas period – "we had to lock the doors on Christmas Eve, we simply could not get another body in the place" – this means some desperately lonely wet winter Monday lunchtimes, and lots of time to worry about how on earth the bills are going to be paid. Remember that no matter how many customers you have, your costs in the winter will be very little different from summer: you may be able to trim staff costs in winter, but electricity and heating will be higher, while your income could be half in February what it is in August.

However, do also bear in mind that with the increase in leisure time for many, especially older people, and the seeming trend towards milder winters, more people are travelling out to pubs in the winter. Can you do something to help attract this very valuable trade?

Handy Tip Eighteen

If the pub you are buying is highly seasonal, beware of moving in at any time of the year other than early spring. If you move in in summer you will have no time to learn the ropes while being snowed under with caravanners. In autumn you will have five or six months of loss to face, which will eat into reserves, while you will also have to cope with customers' expectations regarding your Christmas hospitality plans.

The cash-flow predictions which your business plan will show should, if at all possible, be prepared on one of the very cheap, easy to use and comprehensive spreadsheet computer programs which are widely available for PCs and Apple Macintosh computers. (You will certainly need a home computer of this kind!)

The spreadsheet will enable you to look at your cash flow and profitability well into the future, and if the figures entered into the program are reasonably accurate, then so will be the outcome, hence the need to research all costs and income carefully.

Then, when you come to start trading yourself, you can track your progress compared with these predictions, and replace estimated costs and income with real ones, thus giving you a much better prediction of the state of your finances in the months to come. This

This means some desperately lonely wet winter Monday lunchtimes, and lots of time to worry about how on earth the bills are going to be paid.

will give you a very useful, if not essential, forewarning of rags or riches, and you can act accordingly. The spreadsheet will also tell you the long-term effects of any proposed changes – the introduction of a Quiz Night or Dance Evening, for example – provided your estimates of costs and income prove correct in long-term practice.

Handy Tip Nineteen

You might feel that having a singer or "popular beat combo" will help boost trade on, say, a Thursday night. Assuming you have all the right licences, (for details of which you should consult a book more designed to tell you how to run a pub rather than how to buy one, your consultant or your solicitor), it might well cost you £250 to lay on this event. Allow not only for the group's fee but also the cost of advertising and even any extra power, or food (or even beer!) the group might consume, not to mention extra bar or catering staff.

As noted above, in a leasehold pub you will need to take at least £2500 over the bar to cover this investment, perhaps £1500 in a freehold operation. That is an awful lot of extra pints of beer, a level of drinking you may find hard to cater for, even if you can find the staff to serve them and the place to stand the drinkers. And, of course, miserable oldies like yours truly might be so horrified by the unaccustomed noise that they take their long-term custom elsewhere.

Such events are rarely profitable in the size of pub you are likely to run, unless you have the ability to charge separately for entrance to the "function room". At best they are a service to the community, which might be appreciated if there is "nowt else to do", and at worst an awful lot of trouble if your idea of a popular beat combo is not shared by as many folk as you had hoped. Not everyone can arrange a Wigan Casino All-Nighter!

SCENE THREE:

ENTERING THE FINAL LAP

With a bid made and accepted, your training under your belt, the business plan written and refined, and all your advisers fully appraised of your plans and duly behind you, things will move ahead in a similar way to a house purchase, with a few notable additions.

If you are buying a freehold it ought to be straightforward, and your solicitor will discuss with you in detail any points that arise through the normal searches, and whether, for example, there are any covenants or restrictions on the property which affect you.

One major task is to have the property surveyed by a fully qualified professional experienced in surveying commercial properties. Such experts are found by personal recommendation, through estate agents or the *Yellow Pages* and similar directories, and a proper survey may well cost £1000. Most pubs are old buildings, some are very old, and if you are buying freehold and it really is the pub of your dreams, you may decide to let certain deficiencies go unattended to in your keenness to be the landlord. That is a gamble only you can judge whether to take, for your buyer, come the time, might not be as

Miserable oldies like yours truly might be so horrified by the unaccustomed noise that they take their long-term custom elsewhere.

generous. And the fault, whatever it is, will not have got any better of its own accord over the years.

The situation is different for a leasehold pub: almost certainly the lease will be "fully repairing", which means the tenant has to put right at his own expense anything and everything that needs putting right, and the landlord (brewery) will have the building regularly inspected for new or unrectified faults. If you have to do repairs when and to the standard demanded by the brewery, it could eat heavily into your already slim profits, especially if it is something like woodworm or dry rot doing the eating.

So be very careful with your survey, especially if it is a leased pub, and ensure that the outgoing landlord fixes every fault found before you exchange contracts, and that the brewery is fully satisfied that the building is in 100% order. The last thing you want is the brewery turning up after you have been in a week saying it is now your responsibility to have a new roof built, which £10,000 task Old Harry was meant to do three years ago. You need to obtain from the brewery a properly authorised letter saying that, at the date of exchange of contracts there was no outstanding work to be done in relation to the fully-repairing aspects of the lease.

And do ensure you have a full insurance policy in place from changeover day, so that any damage caused can be repaired at the insurance company's expense. There are specialist policies covering pubs, and it is essential that you get the right policy in place from the moment you take over, or you could be facing more unnecessary and possibly crippling expense. (And this is another cost, perhaps £2000 or more, unless you can pay in instalments over the year, that you will have to budget for paying, before you have taken a penny over the bar.)

Visit, or at the very least talk at length over the phone with the relevant council Planning Department. Make sure there are no problems in principle with any embryonic plans you might have to change the buildings. Get to know the local procedures, whether the building is in a conservation area or is listed, and whether there have been any plans submitted in the past that have been rejected (and why) or are still active. One town where we nearly bought a pub – and I am sure this is indeed normal – required planning permission even for a temporary sign, and it takes at least six weeks for an application to be considered. We wanted to erect a sign "Opening Soon", but we had to apply for permission – cost £50 – and we would have been open long before the application had been heard. Erection of banners such as "Barbecue here next Sunday" are totally impossible in such regimes. Similarly, the fixing of new pub-name signs and lighting to the building (both temporary ones while proper ones were being made) – needed permission, as did the covering over of part of two steps to make an access ramp for wheelchairs. Planning is a law unto itself, and the local whys and wherefores need to be understood before you cross the path of the chairman of the planning committee.

Getting and keeping accounts

This is the biggest Catch 22 of them all, and to help you navigate through this minefield you will certainly need a good accountant with relevant experience

No-one buys a business without having carefully analysed at least three years' solid trading accounts duly certified as being accurate: that is unless you have so much money, so little sense or are so carefree that the past trading history of the business, be it a railway company, an engineering works, a coal mine or a humble local pub, is of no concern. If your plan is to demolish the pub, erect a dozen executive homes and make a half million profit, then ten thousand here or there may not worry you, even though it should.

So you need to see proper accounts before you go any further.

The trouble is, it does seem that not all publicans keep accounts of any quality – it is one of those jobs that is not really necessary, they perhaps feel, a chore of even greater dread than changing barrels or cleaning the toilets. And as for many years on end they have had no intention of selling up, they keep the barest of financial information and blunder their way through the Inland Revenue's demands for money.

And it has to be said that under the recent legislation for income tax self-assessment, there is no legal need for a pub run as a sole trader or partnership business to keep accounts, even though filling in the form properly and paying only the minimum tax called for is rather dependent on accurate back-up information!

And then comes the fateful day when the brewery raises the rent beyond Tolerance Point, the local factory closes and all your customers are made redundant, or your partner gets ill, pregnant or arrested, and you have to sell up.

No accounts? No problem, it's easy to find an unscrupulous accountant to invent some for you, at a price (Joke!! All accountants are totally honest!)

But then along comes a buyer, like you, who is very keen to start on the right track and firstly get, and then keep for himself, proper accounts. As a layman, it is easy to spot a fake once you have seen half a dozen good sets of accounts, and a decent accountant can spot the dud while it is still inside the envelope in the postman's bag!

If a pub has no proper accounts, be very very wary. You can only really judge the proper price to pay if you know what profit has been made over the past three years, at least, and the implications thereon of, for example, rent rises or new licensing laws. You may well be able to sense fairly accurately the likely turnover from visiting the pub on several occasions and counting the heads and calculating the likely takings, but that gives no true picture of the overall profitability.

From proper accounts you will also be able to see where you might be able to make savings, and hence better profits. Some pages ago I remarked on two ostensibly similar pubs whose accounts showed very different telephone costs. One had rock solid accounts that positively gleamed excellence, the others were less impressive. You should check each line item, consider if you can do better, by tighter controls or shopping around, and feed that change into your business plan. Without proper accounts your business plan is only a weak guess.

So don't let your heart rule your mind at this stage. You have come a long way to get this far, and are very close to pulling your first pint, don't throw away all that conscientious labour because the roses above the door lure you strongly in the face of dodgy accounting information. Don't be afraid to withdraw your offer if proper accounts, that is accounts to your accountant's satisfaction, are not provided as a matter of course.

Even good accounts can conceal a hidden problem – bank interest or management charges, for example, might hide a loan or other financial problems that are not obvious. Low building repair costs could be camouflage for a big problem covered over with a coat of paint. Are the large costs under "motor" a true reflection of the distance and frequency of travel to the local cash and carry, and of the vehicle parked in the garage?

And when you have bought the business which had the good accounts, keep them that way, religiously. It is a far better investment to put effort into weekly analyses, monthly management accounts and quarterly trading statistics, and employ an extra bar staff member to cover for you, than the other way around. After all, apart from the absolute need to know how the business is going, and to pay only the least tax possible, someone just like you will one day want to buy the business from you, and will want to see those gleaming accounts: you will get the investment you have made in keeping proper accounts many times over by way of an easier sale and a better selling price!

THE CURTAIN FALLS – CHANGEOVER DAY

The day when you take over and move in, and the old landlord, his wife and family, his goods and chattels but hopefully none of his customers, move out, is called changeover day.

This is where our experience runs out. Once Viv was a licensee of a closed pub we never opened, twice we had offers to purchase accepted but later withdrew, never did we get to actually pulling our first pint, so this short, closing section relates how we viewed the last hurdle we never reached.

You almost certainly know how stressful a domestic house move can be, especially under the vagaries of English law. Think of that, and at least triple the aggravation, stress and chaos, not to mention the number of things to do in a set time, and you are getting somewhere near our view of the impending changeover.

In a domestic house move it is usual to time completion of the sale of your house with the purchase of your new one, and of all the other sales and purchases in the chain. Last minute delays are also common as someone plays silly b's and demands more money or more time. For some reason known only to themselves, many people take on a whole new persona when moving house: doubtless it applies to pubs. So I would suggest you try and decouple the whole thing.

If you have to sell your house to raise the money to buy the pub, it is probable that the bank may not be too keen on an open-ended bridging loan, a reluctance they may display by asking for a very high interest rate to cover the loan. And in any case borrowing the money at three or four per cent over base puts a hefty strain on the cash-flow in the early days and is to be avoided. You would be very unwise to attempt to buy a pub if your house is not even under offer – one thing at a time!

So, if at all possible, sell any property you need to sell before you buy the pub, and then go live in a rented house, sensibly as close to the pub as possible, while the pub purchase goes through. If it falls down and you end up buying somewhere else, then of course this is less than ideal!!

The outgoing landlord may be retiring, and going off to his new villa in Spain, in which case he may be very flexible in his preferred moving out date, or he may be moving to another pub, with all the added complications of a "double shuffle". Take into account at this stage – preferably before – any possible last minute delays which might be caused by, for example, the brewery's requirement for training or for repairs to be done to comply with either the lease or your own demands of the outgoing landlord. Do not be rushed or try and stick to deadlines or to cut corners or accept second best – there will be problems to be overcome and frustrations to be endured right up to the last minute.

Either way, when you finally come to move in you have to co-ordinate the moving of your furniture and effects from wherever they are to the pub, and, as with a domestic move, time your effects' arrival with the departure of the outgoing landlord's.

At the same time, you need to be at the pub with the landlord, and, usually, an independent stock-taker, to go through all the items being left behind in the pub, by which I mean all drinks and food products, and possibly glasses and breakable catering items, and value them. On the one hand the landlord may have run down his stocks so as to

Low building repair costs could be camouflage for a big problem covered over with a coat of paint.

minimise his outgoings: on the other you will want him to have ordered up good stocks, so you are not faced with empty barrels or optics on Day Two.

Whichever, you have stock to value and a price to agree, and it is not unknown for the outgoing landlord to demand cash for the agreed amount before you get the keys – although it is customary for both parties to agree the stock-taker's valuation without argument. Of course, you hope you will have negotiated things in a more friendly atmosphere, but this is one way the vendor can get revenge if you have upset him along the way.

Morning opening time is now fast-approaching, and someone has to take responsibility for opening up, putting a float in the tills, ensuring all the rostered staff arrive properly (and making emergency arrangements if not), ensuring the bar and all menus, signs and products are properly displayed, and that the kitchen is in top gear and ready to churn out its usual delicacies. No customer entering the bar must realise that a changeover is going on. Closing for the day is not really an option in these days of fierce competition and fickle loyalties.

Amid all this, if you are lucky, the kids will need taking to and from school, feeding or whatever, according to their ages. Clearly, it is a very good idea to employ a relief manager to look after the pub for you while this is all going on and for the next few days while you get settled and find where you have packed the tranquillisers.

Then comes the biggie. Licensing law, as you have found out on your training courses and are about to find out for real, is plain daft in many cases, or at best archaic.

On changeover day whoever is to be licensee – that is one, both or all of a team – have to go, along with the outgoing licensee, and stand in front of a local magistrate and apply for a Protection Order. This allows you to trade as a licensee pending a more formal hearing, and absolves the outgoing from any further responsibilities with regard to the licensed premises.

So, just to be clear, you are hoping that completion comes through on time so the property is yours, supervising the furniture move, arranging and motivating staff, valuing and paying for the stock and

. . . .

opening the doors, all simultaneously – AND you have to go to the local court, which may be some miles distant, and see the magistrate.

A good trick if you can do it, but thousands of landlords have done it before, and it is good initiation into what is to follow in the months ahead.

At the Protection Order hearing, which of course is at a time of the magistrates' convenience and may be altered to suit the court and not you, the police have the power to object to the transfer and stop you being granted the licence and moving in. Hence why you should have spoken to them weeks ago and made sure there was no just impediment. Imagine, by the time of the hearing you are almost certainly the legal owner of the building, or its lease, and suddenly PC Smith stands up, bows to the court and reveals your past convictions for drunkenness and hitting a magistrate… the implications are horrendous. Of course, if he has been on the ball, your solicitor will have made sure that the exchange of contracts, and hence the purchase, will have been conditional on the Protection Order being granted, and you will have taken advice to ensure no objection was likely to be forthcoming, but this is the crunch moment!!

And then you walk out of the court with your Protection Order, a licensee at last, only to find…. well you can imagine the many things that might have gone wrong while you have all been sitting in the waiting room at the court building.

You are now on your own. The pub will be open and trading when you get back, and the man can come round and put your name over the door. You can introduce your menus, your signs and your ways of doing things. You can hire and fire the staff, get rid of the bouncy castle, install widescreen TV. You must keep records for the VAT man and the income tax man, and keep close track of all stock to ensure proper and efficient ordering. You must also stay abreast of the law – not just licensing, but health and safety and employment as well, not to mention local planning regulations. You can run the business – your business – the way you want to do and sink or swim by your own efforts, helped of course by those nice people at the brewery and those really nice people who are your consultants. You can even exercise the full majesty of the law by excluding people from the bar as you choose. It is your house, your public house.

. . . .

But you may not serve alcoholic drink to a police officer, unless authorised to do so by his superior, nor to a known prostitute seeking business.

Good luck. We never got that far, so we cannot say whether we think it is fun or not, but it is certainly bloody hard work.

ON THE WAY OUT OF THE AUDITORIUM

"Patrons may leave by all the exit doors and all such doors must be opened and clearly sign-posted" – consider an alternative, always leave a way out freely available.

A home from home

So, you really want to buy a pub and live in a lovely building in your part of the country, BUT, having considered this book and many other sources of information as well, now you are not quite so sure.

Well, you could buy a pub and convert it into your dream home...

It is becoming more of a trend. Especially in the south of England, where trade is more affected by imports of cheap booze from the continent, and where house prices are very much higher than in the north, the asking price of a pub, even one trading well and with good accounts, may well be significantly lower than you would have to pay for a private house of similar dimensions. And if the pub is suffering through fierce competition, through the importation problems, or simply because the village it is in is a dying one and there is little local or drive-to trade (don't forget the presumed impact of drink-drive laws on public house trade!!), the differential will be even greater. And the pub may well have a car park or large beer garden on which you might be able to build another house, to sell for a profit. In any case, pub prices are often depressed by the large pub-owning breweries selling off a hundred or more outlets in one tranche, so as to implement new corporate policy or keep within government anti-monopoly regulations, so while private house prices

But you may not serve alcoholic drink to a police officer, unless authorised to do so by his superior, nor to a known prostitute seeking business.

in some parts of the country continue to rise strongly, public house ones can be seen to decline!

And, while there are some 65,000 public houses in the UK, the industry itself thinks that is 10,000 too many to support the trade which is declining through the changing patterns of British social life – so as many as ten per cent of pub sales are going to people whose aim is to close the pub and either live in it or develop the site.

There are possibly four snags to this route. First you will need change-of-use planning permission from the local council, and if it is a council intent on stopping the decline in rural services it might be contrary to its policy to grant such an application. But there are always ways and means with Planning!

Then, if it is in the Green Belt or a Conservation Area, or if it is a Listed Building, for example, there might well be firmer restrictions regarding development.

Thirdly, if it is a pub with a generous parcel of land, bigger developers might be in the frame, with plans to demolish the pub and build several new houses on the site.

And finally, there might be the reaction of the locals to the loss of their watering hole – you might not be too popular if you close the best pub for miles!

But, it has been known for a pub to be sold for under £200,000, converted into a private house for perhaps £50,000 and then be worth well over £400,000.... A tempting route, and one which will become ever more popular as the private landlord faces ever increasing threats to his livelihood.

Strike the Set

. . . .

THE PUB SAGA

BEING A HISTORY OF STEVE AND VIV'S ATTEMPTS TO BUY A PUB

Origins

From the day we started pub-hunting we kept a blow-by-blow diary, not realising, of course, that the end would see us not in a pub at all. This is basically the diary as written, edited only to remove the names and identities of those persons and companies best not mentioned, and largely put into the past tense to make for easier reading. Additionally, some retrospective comments were added during the preparation of this book to help (hopefully) the reader understand what was happening.

It is, by its very nature, a personal account, even a sob-story perhaps, and our readers are asked to allow for any personal emotion which shows through! It does illustrate, we think, how two educated, bright and industrious people can go sadly astray, even though they were being fastidious to ensure they were surrounded by all the right advice.

First steps

To begin at the beginning is hard, for like all things this project just grew. To go back to where we come from or how we met is to go back too far, yet there is no firm start, only a development of a germ of an idea. That's how most things start, isn't it?

. . . .

The best place to start is perhaps Christmas 1996. Things seemed to be set fair for us, and although our publishing business, which we had run together for almost ten years, was faltering, a brainstorm over the holidays came up with a number of viable projects. Indeed we surmised that if they all came off we would have too much to do!! Viv knew she would be busy with her report work for a company in Wimbledon, and I (Steve) had my writing work for a major aerospace company and work on a monthly aerospace newsletter we ran with our very best friends and business partners.

Among the new projects were: the creation of a major directory of complementary medicine, the launch of a magazine and/or a series of books on railway history, the use of our house as a photo venue, and the development of a management magazine – enough to keep us busy and maybe keep us solvent....

The first major blow occurred at 10.30pm on 10 January 1997. Rather like knowing exactly what you were doing when President Kennedy was shot, this is a moment etched on the memory. We received a fax, out of the blue and without rhyme or reason, from the aforementioned friends saying they were pulling out of the newsletter and of our little company. They cut all links immediately and without explanation, and threw us into turmoil. Any chance of developing those activities went in a flash, and with it a good part of our hopes for the new year.

We still saw no reason at all to change course but as the spring progressed the publishing ideas we had set in train all slowly vanished for a variety of reasons. At the same time Viv was very busy, and was heading for Paris for two weeks' work in mid-June, but after that we could see a huge hole, and with none of the new projects progressing things suddenly looked bleak!

It slowly dawned on us that we were flogging a dead horse as far as publishing was concerned, and that the only sensible way ahead was to do something entirely new. Quite when and how it was that this light broke on us I'm not sure, but it became blindingly obvious that if we did not do something drastic we would be in serious financial difficulties before the end of the year. As we discussed the ideas and possibilities, we realised how many people had dropped manure on us over the years – they were never going to work with us again and the chances of finding new clients were slim, given the way we work and the way technology has leapt forward since we started. No use crying over spilt milk, so to speak, tread boldly was the slogan....

So, what could we do? We had our brains and personalities, a lot of computer equipment, ten years' experience running a business, and perhaps £300,000 net assets tied up in three houses – and not a penny spare in the bank!! We had to find something we could do mentally – no point in trying to become a brain surgeon or airline pilot – and physically – I have poor eyesight and Viv is of slim stature, so that rules a lot out as well. Given the love we have for good beer, ironically imbued in us by the now-departed friends, we quickly realised that owning a pub was about the only thing we could physically do and had the enthusiasm and mental skills, if not the direct experience, to do.

An early plan was to start small and to buy a café of some sort, leaving us time to do the remnants of our publishing. Steve's friend from primary school days, Graham Tillotson, (who makes a repeat cameo appearance at the end of this saga) had just made a successful transition from civil engineer to fish-and-chip shop owner, and his success and happiness in his new trade concentrated our minds. Then we thought that a part-time cafe just would not work, nor did it make sense financially, so we decided to go for broke – a total switch to a pub, or nothing.

Our first copy of *The Publican* newspaper was dated 28 April 1997. Just five weeks before we had moved my elderly father from North Yorkshire to Bury, convinced we would be staying here for a very long time – we had changed course very rapidly. Within a couple of weeks we saw two adverts which changed our lives – one was for a pub, referred to in this book as Pub One, and the other had been placed by a company offering training courses.

We took *The Publican* regularly and it proved an excellent source of information and of "pubs for sale" adverts, and soon we read of a fair few freehold sales which were seemingly affordable and gave us the likelihood of making a decent living. We ruled out all options except buying a freehold freehouse, as being the only way to be in charge of our own destinies. We made the decision to go for it, to put our house on the market and hope we would find an acceptable pub in the right time frame. We contacted all the estate agents advertising in *The Publican*, giving ourselves a fairly wide geographical band, from beyond Ripon and Leeds in the east and then westwards almost to the Fylde coast, and sat back to wait for the agents' leaflets to arrive.

First hurdles

We consulted the bank, and on 7 June had our first meeting with the training company (henceforth referred to as the consultancy, because that is what they soon became). We got on very well with the representative who came to see us, an avuncular and jovial publican with both experience and enthusiasm, not to mention genuine keenness to take us on board as one of the consultancy's first clients.

One important reconnaissance was made – Steve visited the new landlord who was the consultancy's first client to be "installed" in a pub. He was very supportive and very complimentary about the consultancy's services, so we were more confident our choice was going to be a good one.

A contract was signed with the consultancy within a week, not just for training, but for the total package which also included finding us our ideal pub and helping us in every way to buy and operate it and be successful. Finding this firm was certainly a very good move, we would not have got anywhere without them – (remember, this part of the book is being written diary fashion in real time, so there's no telling how far we will get), but we soon passed where we would have been without them!!

We put our own house on the market – the house we love so much and from where I always had said the only way I would leave would be to carry me out in a box. But the asking price suggested by the agent was very acceptable and gave us more room for manoeuvre.

Of all the pubs we saw advertised at this early stage, very few came within our geographic area – there were lots just outside, but Pub One was just about the only one inside which also met our financial criteria. We told the consultant of our interest and he immediately contacted the selling agent, obtained the details and went and saw it himself (as it was far closer to him than to us), only to report back that it was closed and boarded up.

Intrigued, Steve visited the site himself while Viv was in Paris on 16 June. The fact that the pub was once a railway station did not bear on what followed at all (Steve admits to a passing interest in railways but does not have an anorak!), but it was immediately clear that although this was not the charming village pub with climbing roses and a canal alongside that we might have already dreamt of, it was going to be unbeatable in its location and as a challenge.

The next two weeks were frustrating – weren't they all? We wanted to bid for Pub One, but found the system hard to crack. The pub was owned by a brewery (who were selling the freehold free of tie), and there wasn't a clear line through the agent to anyone making a decision – and we found it hard to get a response. (While it had taken less than two weeks for us to find the consultant, check him out, sign the contract and locate and visit the pub site, it was another six weeks before any further progress was made, which perhaps ought to have been an omen.)

Cutting a long story short, the pub's owners (Brewery 1) would not consider our bid for the freehold, let alone accept until we had proven we had the finance – and it made no difference that we had so much collateral tied up in our houses. So, having put our formal bid in via the consultant on 15 July, we finally met at the consultant's office on 6 August with representatives of another brewery (Brewery 2) who were seemingly keen to lend us the money needed to buy the pub until such time as we had sold our house. Brewery 2 said they would lend us the asking price, on condition we would accept a tie to their beer, and it appeared to us from what the consultant said that the effective interest rate to be charged was very low indeed. In other words it appeared as if "2" was lending us the money, and I do emphasise the word "lend" as it would have got it all back as soon as we had sold our house, at virtually zero interest, in return for getting its beers into a substantial public house in new territory. So in our naivety we verbally accepted this offer. If only we had known the truth this might well have been the end of this diary!

Convoluted responses

That sparked, albeit slowly, Brewery 1 into action, for it suddenly realised that it was selling a pub it owned but was allowing a competitor to supply the beer. It immediately changed its tune and, after the consultant's MD had met with one of its directors, it said it would only sell the pub to us if we sold its beer, and it would "lend" us the money to enable the purchase to go ahead: they would not entertain the deal made with Brewery 2. We formally met with Brewery 1 on 15 August, and although the deal was not as good as we thought it would be, it was pretty fair, so we went ahead – we had every confidence we would soon sell our house and have no need of any loan.

(Strangely, in retrospect, Brewery 1 would not sell us the pub without this tie, which we think ought to be illegal, and it transpired on further inquiry that 2's offer was nothing like as good in reality as we had been led to believe – perhaps, to be generous we had jumped to an optimistic conclusion in our haste to proceed. In essence Brewery 1 said it would lend us £165,000 out of a total agreed price of £195,000, with an interest rate set at 3% over the Bank of England base rate and with the capital to be repaid in equal instalments spread over ten years. We would be tied to its beers, as with a leased pub, but unlike a leased pub we would get discounts off the list prices. In order to be able to justify the loan internally, the representative had said we would sell 350 barrels of beer a year: we pointed out that even after we had got ourselves established we were only aiming at 200, but he assured us this figure of 350 was only for internal reasons and would have no effect on us in practise, even if we sold no beer at all.)

The following week it all started to happen, with a vengeance (oh, in the meantime we had had our first two days training, in Hygiene and Licensing Law, and, of course, we passed with hardly a mark dropped!)

A most excellent meeting was had with our bank manager, Doug, (at the branch nearest the pub) on 19 August, followed by one with the agents through whom we were renting out a house, who said we could put it up for sale in January 1998 rather than the summer of 1999 as we had been planning: this would help long-term financing a great deal.

If we were moving from Bury, Steve's dad wanted to go back to Yorkshire, so we put dad's new house on the market on 21 August, thinking it would take weeks and we could move into the pub and then move dad. Of course, Sod's Law being what it is, we got an offer, showing us a small profit on the deal, two days later. Dad started packing immediately, he could not wait to be back in Yorkshire!! (Ironically, Pub One is only about three miles from where dad had moved only a few weeks before all this started.)

We also met with Amanda, the elder daughter of one of Steve's cousins and who lived just a 15 minute drive from Pub One. She has masses of experience in pubs, even more enthusiasm and was very keen to help, and later we asked her to become our "weekends manager", for starters.

So, as of 27 August 1997, (when all the previous text was originally written) we are waiting for the loan to be processed by the owners, and when it is approved we can put things into the hands of the solicitors. We are forging ahead with plans for training and all sorts of ideas for the pub. Steve's dad is out house-hunting and one family has been to view our own house four times, they must be close to making an offer! The tension is unbearable!! The loan we will need is huge, and the payments a real millstone, but if we can sell this house we won't need one! We feel the challenge of opening the pub, on the presently planned date of 8 November, is daunting to say the least!

The saga now moves forward to the next diary entry, dated 29 October 1997

Downhill fast

All has not gone according to plan in the past two months – Dad is moving, but we are not!!

To deal with Dad first, we soon found him a lovely new house in a Dales village where he spent many childhood holidays, and, although the purchase has taken longer than hoped, as they always do, he is moving next Friday, 7 November, all being well.

A major activity on the pub front was the training we had, a very intensive week in Wakefield. As might have been expected by anyone who knows her, Viv was top student, taking it very seriously, and I was pleased I did well given that I cannot see well enough to read notes. We subsequently both got our British Institute of Innkeepers certificates which are necessary to get an on-licence.

Back at Pub One we had all sorts of hassle, of which what follows is only a sample. Firstly the consultant's MD volunteered to use one of his mates to get us quotes for all the refurbishment work needed, which we had estimated at £30,000 by the very roughest of guesses.

(Remember, the pub was closed and boarded up when we first saw it: it had been closed for some time, the managing landlord having, so it was said, "done a runner", even leaving the last session's washing up in the sink. A great deal was needed to make the public areas attractive, while the whole of the living accommodation needed re-modelling.)

After waiting almost a month for these quotes – the chap had not turned up on site when we had gone to meet him there so he got off to a bad start anyway – we became quite animated at the delays being incurred by this total lack of service. During our training week the MD told us he had actually received quite a few written quotes but was holding them back until he had the lot, a policy we could not quite understand at the time. The MD's secretary followed this up by phoning us to say the good news was that many of these quotes were under the preliminary budget and that we were already £1000 "to the good". Yet delay followed delay until eventually the MD admitted his mate had done nothing and the quotes never existed. So, a full month after we had been told this chap was taking care of the quotes nothing had been achieved and we had to do it all ourselves from scratch.

So we spent three days on site briefing would-be contractors and getting quotes. Not totally surprisingly these were far more than the "friend" had estimated. Although he had provided no quotes obtained from suppliers, he had done a rough run through with a supposedly professional eye and had come up with a grand total of £29,774 – remarkably close to my guess of £30,000, and I have absolutely no experience of building work whatsoever!! (In retrospect I should have been very suspicious of this and realised what was going on.) But when we got REAL quotes none were within 30% of the "friend's" estimates and many were two or three times more. Even to do the bare minimum before opening would have cost £40,000 to £50,000.

The more we saw of Pub One, though, the more we felt at home and the more we pressed on. The potential was huge and everyone we spoke to was most enthusiastic. The bank was especially helpful, agreeing that the £30,000 we needed as balance for the purchase, plus capital for the refurbishment, would be available at 24 hours' notice.

Viv had a meeting to start the ball rolling on catering, and we got down to designing our business letterheads, a newsletter to announce our plans to the locals and other material we would need to market the pub as soon as we had the keys.

Shock waves

Then the first Big Shock arrived early in October, when, on exactly the date the representative had said it would be when we had agreed the offer face-to-face six weeks earlier, the owner's financial offer letter arrived, and it was truly a bombshell. The story is best told in the letter I subsequently sent to the consultants, but in short the three-page brewery letter contained nine conditions we had not heard of before and which were unacceptable. It was crystal clear that no-one at Brewery 1 was going to offer any goodwill towards our efforts to buy their pub, but worse was to come!!

On 8 October we met with a more senior manager from Brewery 1 and had a very heated conversation. At one point I closed my briefcase and stood up to leave, ending the discussions and walking away from the deal, but he agreed to amend several points and we accepted others which did not really affect us. Off I went thinking, "OK, bad deal, but nothing that affects us after we have sold this house so it will all go away after that."

Some of the nine conditions are noted below, as they may be of help to readers faced with similar conflicts between what a brewery representative says and what appears in writing – remember we are buying a freehold pub which has been closed for many months, and the owners owed others a considerable sum of money which our purchase would help pay off.

1: The loan rate was to be 4% above base if we failed to reach 350 barrels a year, which 'target' we had agreed with the brewery rep was unattainable. This meant payments of £1400 a month. (The verbal agreement had been 3 over base, with no link to the amount of beer sold.)

2: The minimum trading commitment was 350 barrels/year. Below that figure we would lose discount on barrels on a barrel-for-barrel basis – this is known as a shortfall charge. In other words if we reached our own optimistic target of

200 barrels/year we would have discount on only 50, costing us a further £7500 a year.

3: The owners demanded sight of our accounts annually.

4: all the owners' legal and professional fees would be paid by us, estimated to be at least £5000.

5: The loan was conditional on us carrying out refurbishment worth £37,000 within three months (although, of course, we had to do the refurbishment before opening to make the place habitable!)

6: The capital would be repaid over ten years – a charge of £1400 a month. This meant the total repayments would be £3400 a month, more than our anticipated gross takings in the first few weeks!

7: The owners reserved the right to terminate the loan with three months' notice, which would have left us with no pub!!

(And again remember, the brewery was selling a pub which had not been trading for some time, and on which they owed other parties money. You might have thought they would be quite keen to see a sale and the debts paid off...)

The financial saga August-October 1997

This is an edited version of the letter I sent to our consultants as a summary of this period on 17 October. I regret that having to change the name of the brewery to "owners" and the name of the area manager to "rep" makes this section harder to read.)

Dear Consultant

As we appear to be over one difficult phase and into the next, we thought we should put on the record the saga with regard to the financing of Pub One... the whole sorry business is one we have learned a lot of lessons from. Maybe if we record our thoughts at this stage it will serve as a lesson for others who follow us.

Additionally, we would like to place on the record some feelings which we have not previously expressed.

When we saw Pub One advertised we thought that in terms of location and potential it was probably unbeatable, and, heartened by your enthusiasm for the challenge we put in a bid shortly after we had first seen the advert.

It then became clear that a bid of £165,000 was not going to be entertained, for although the pub had effectively been on the market for four years and was standing derelict and empty, there was "strong interest" from others. So, we decided we wanted to bid the full asking price in order to be assured of success, taking the view that in the long term £10,000 either way was not significant, and that a full-price bid would result in more goodwill from the vendor, as is the case when buying a house.

Clearly, one doesn't make a bid for anything without the requisite funds available, but we were taken aback that for the owners to take us seriously, even at full price, we had immediately to prove we had finance. We had the assets to give us the security for the bid, but had been planning on providing the proof on exchange of contracts, as would be normal.

Then we were told that another brewery *(referred to as Brewery 2 in the above book text)* was interested in supporting us, and along came two of its men, clearly keen to do a deal. Both Viv and I believed, after that meeting, that that brewery's deal was for a loan of £165,000 at 0.9% interest rate. Now we will charitably say this, and a number of other points, were genuine misunderstandings on our part, being naive, but it must be statistically quite improbable that two people misinterpret more than one conversation wrongly in exactly the same way. Since the offer was available immediately and was clearly better than we could do commercially, we put aside our personal efforts in this regard and concentrated on securing the funding for the remaining sum we would need before the sale of our house. (This was settled in one short meeting and is available on 24 hours' notice, in stark contrast to what followed with the owners.) Had we gone our route, or Brewery 2's, we would have been trading by now.

And at this stage we bid the full price, backed by Brewery 2, through the correct channel, i.e. the selling estate agents.

Then the owners woke up to what was going on, and said in order for our bid to be accepted we had to have their finance and their beer. Our solicitor advised us that such a condition "was probably illegal, and certainly immoral", but we were cornered, we had to agree to it if we wanted the pub, and we did. And at this stage someone put the agent's nose out of joint by by-passing them, and this led to continuing bad-feeling from them, which culminated in a hostile letter faxed from the agent late last Friday – totally unnecessary and ill-will we had no part in yet which fell on us.

It may well be that the owner interpreted our ready acceptance of both price and tie as one of weakness, and decided to take further advantage. We, on the other hand, were thinking that friendliness here would result in friendliness in return. The owner has certainly viewed us as a very soft touch, and probably mentally deficient as well.

At the meeting where the owner put its offer of finance forward, its rep specifically said he had proposed we would sell 350 barrels a year, as that figure was needed to justify the loan, and, in turn, the price they were asking for the derelict hulk of a building. He also categorically said in response to a specific question that no penalty would accrue if we did not reach that level, that all the discounts would remain untouched no matter what level of sales we reached, and that he did not expect us to reach 350 – it was, plain and simple, a figure to justify the loan on the owner's own internal criteria.

We discussed the owner's conditions – an interest rate of 3% over base, capital repayments over ten years, etc., with our advisers, all of whom have experience of the licensed trade. To a man they were vehement that it was bad deal and that we should negotiate it down. Not one of the five expressed a view that the deal was anything other than a rip off – "rooked" and "crap" were the two simplest quotes. And fair enough, as soon as I mentioned this to the rep he conceded a three-month moratorium on interest and capital, not ideal but at least a step. Yes, you, who know far more than the others, advised us it was a good deal, and we accepted it, but the actual figures are not relevant – whether it is 2 or 4 per cent above base makes little actual difference, it is the total lack of goodwill which so totally stuns us. "Customer care" is simply not in the owner's vocabulary when it comes to dealing with landlords.

Anyway, six weeks later, the owner's offer letter duly appeared, and it was totally different from what had been agreed verbally, the now famous "nine points". In particular, it was an interest rate four over base and a £50/barrel penalty for any shortfall below 350 barrels/ year.

I complained strongly to the rep about this, saying no-one expected us to sell 350/year, least of all us. He replied by saying "it's in your business plan, so surely you plan on selling that much. We cannot agree the loan without that being achieved."

Despite my anger, I was dumbstruck – 350/year was HIS idea and HE had said we wouldn't be expected to get that high! And, of course, we have yet to produce a business plan, so goodness knows where he got that idea from. He agreed to defer the penalty for one year, but it still hangs over us.

Let us look at that 350 figure. In the outline plan you have drawn up we are looking at doing £3500/ week wet takings. Since we plan on heavily promoting wines and spirits, I estimate that £3500/week equates to, generously, 240 barrels/year, a target I shall be delighted if we reach eventually. No way is the place going to sell more. And from the figures we have for trading in 1994 it was doing perhaps 100 barrels/year then, so anything above that is an improvement.

For the rep to first suggest 350/year as an unreachable trading figure so he could justify the loan internally and then to come back to us saying the figure was a trading minimum below which we would be penalised barrel-for-barrel is quite, quite unbelievable.

As I say, the owner's philosophy is on another planet. With not one ounce of goodwill shown and penalties like this, a "rip-off" interest rate, etc. etc., how do they expect to hold our custom once the loan is repaid? I have said to the rep that we hope to do business with him over a long period, but he has one heck of a mountain to climb (to re-establish any goodwill).

In different areas – I have no doubt he is saying one thing and then being reined in by someone behind the scenes – the rep has gone back on his word regarding access after we signed the offer letter, (Another "misunderstanding" – the rep said we could have access for refurbishment, at our risk, once we had agreed the offer, his boss then said we had to wait for completion, which would have meant a gap of perhaps a month between completion and our first trading day, with all the incumbent repayment penalties.)

(The brewery's two-faced attitude means that) in reality I don't expect to see the owner's pumps on our bar top for more than a very few weeks....

We now distrust the owners so fundamentally that we are not prepared to rush ahead and do refurbishment until we have examined every clause in both contracts carefully for, having done us once, the idiots at the owners will surely try it on again. What a way to start a business relationship that is supposed to last for years!!

★★

(How prophetic that last paragraph turned out to be, but how naive we were!! Readers might feel "what was the consultant doing all this time? The answer is very little, or so it seems. Our contract with them said they would handle all negotiations with the owners, and we wrote four times underlining that many aspects of the proposed deal were totally unacceptable. We assumed these points were being negotiated on our behalf. Thus when we received the "nine point" letter, we were actually expecting something which took our views into account, not even more unacceptable conditions. The consultant took no part in the meeting with the rep on 8 October, leaving Steve and the rep to slug it out. We should have stopped there and then, but, and let this be a warning, we got far too enthusiastic about things in general and let emotion rule common sense and pragmatism.)

Viv gets a licence

On 15 October Viv stood in front of the local magistrates and got her on-licence – landlady of a pub she never owned, but still confident the owners would eventually be more agreeable on the loan. The sight of a full BII certificate certainly impressed!! The following Friday we met contractors on site for a final briefing, and prepared to move in to do refurbishment as from 27 October, in line with our verbal agreement with the representative.

Then the even bigger bombshells arrived. We returned the offer letter to the owners, detailing the many points we either did not agree with or needed clarification on, and pointing out that what we had agreed with the rep was very different. However, for what became obvious reasons, the owners took this as a formal acceptance of the offer and put it in the hands of their solicitors, who, in line with the agreement we had _not_ signed, started their charges clock ticking.

Clearly everything had been saved up so we would get the really bad news at the very last minute when, they all hoped, it would be too late for us to pull out. Our solicitors got two letters in successive days from the solicitors acting for the owner – one solicitor covered the property transaction, another the finance – note the ability to charge double! On seeing these, with the advice from our solicitor being "pull out now or I resign", we did just that.

We had thought that the so-called 'nine-point, four-page letter' was the formal offer of finance, and that this would be redrafted following our strong comments. But on Monday, 20 October the first of these two letters arrived – the REAL formal offer letter running to ten pages with a further six pages of trading terms. As I noted in a letter of response: "Many of the conditions therein are totally unacceptable some we simply cannot fulfil, others we won't because the answers are no business of the owner's, and others would be simply too expensive to fulfil to be sensible, for example the owner requires us to furnish documents which the owner itself holds – the stupidity of this letter is unbelievable."

The letter also did not amend any of the "nine points" as I had agreed with the rep, and he then confirmed that the owner would not put these changes in writing, only express them verbally, which of course is again totally unacceptable.

So we suspended work on the transaction – yet worse was to come!!

The following day (21 October) our solicitor passed to us the second letter, this one from the owner's "property" solicitor. This included a letter written by the selling estate agent in late-May, only four weeks before we had first expressed an interest, to a company which had just ended negotiations to buy the pub.

(To go back in time, at the very outset the selling agent sent us details of an agreement between Railtrack and Brewery 1, setting out the terms of a licence under which the pub's customers could use the adjacent station car park, and a cost of £4000 a year for this privilege. As no other explanation was offered, we assumed that this was Railtrack seeking to gain income from its property, and we thought that when we were owners we could either renegotiate the deal or simply ask our customers not to park on Railtrack's land.)

The letter we now received gave the real reason why there is this licence. A planning condition, made when the station building was converted into the pub, is that for the pub to operate it must have a certain number of car parking spaces for its sole use during the day, and even more after the evening rush hour has emptied the station car park of commuters' cars, so as to avoid on-street parking and the resultant annoyance to the pub's neighbours. Quite simply, there are not enough available spaces to fulfil either of these conditions, even if there were no commuters' cars parked at all, and the car park is full during the day, so popular is the station. The car park is not big enough to meet the planning conditions and this makes the site unsaleable – insufficient parking means no planning permission, means the on-licence cannot be granted, so there is no pub!! The agent and the owners had been trying all along to sell us – and putting severe obstacles in our way as well – a pub which they knew was in breach of its planning conditions and could not be licensed if the magistrates' court was told the full truth.

(I now return to the actual diary entries.)

So as of today, 29 October 1997, we are licensees of Pub One, although here is little likelihood of us buying it. With the car park situation as it stands the pub is really unsaleable. But as no-one else can buy it without Viv's permission and we cannot accept the owner's financial terms, it is stalemate.

The stress and hassle of the past four months has been unbelievable – no-one would think that a brewery would be so antagonistic towards someone buying a derelict pub from it when there was such a potential for selling its beer – and other advisers have also been less than helpful along the way. We have learned a lot of lessons!!

To bring the story right up to date, yesterday (that is 28 October 1997) we went to see the best pub we have seen advertised since we started looking – even better than Pub One was before we found the problems! Pub Two is a truly splendid freehold pub in a lovely and famous Dales Village – an idyllic setting and maybe this is for us. We drove there with the view to having a meal but it was closed for lunch – just our luck!!

The past four months have been stressful in the extreme, given the position we are in, the next months will be very interesting....

More pubs, more hassle

The diary continues.... It is now 19 February 1998, my dad's 82nd birthday, and things have progressed very little, we are still at our house in Bury.

On the pub front, although Pub Two was idyllic, the bank was not willing to lend us the money needed to buy a freehold pub on the security of our property, because it was uncertain for how long we would need the loan, so we sadly had to let that one go.

(Our involvement with Pub Two was very brief, so there is nothing to relate except our present disappointment. In the main text of this book I mention the need to talk to a bank manager near your intended pub as well as your usual one. In negotiating for Pub One we had done just that, and even set up a business bank account locally. But Pub Two was not in the same area, so we had to travel over 200 miles to our usual branch to discuss our plans from now on, at least until things got firmer – clearly we could not strike up a relationship with every bank manger in whose area we found a possible pub!)

We switch to leasehold

Faced with the unexpected difficulty in raising finance for a freehold pub, even a really good and healthy one, without having sold our house, we then turned our attention more to leasehold pubs, having sought advice from a publican friend of our solicitor in Preston. A leasehold will give us more flexibility and expose less of our capital to risk. And there is more choice.

In early-December we found Pub Three, a leasehold pub in a smart commuter village near Leeds. The location was ideal and the pub itself was very good, although in need of paint. We visited it twice as mystery visitors, had our solicitor check it out in a similar way, made a formal viewing and looked carefully at the area and the competition. It really did look good, with excellent trade, reasonable domestic accommodation, and loads of potential.

However there was an obvious hole in the accounts. Since the latest available set had been published almost 18 months previously, the rent had roughly doubled, and a few weeks of asking failed to elicit either an exact figure or a reason. If the new rent was applied to the old accounts the pub was trading at a significant loss, so we needed better and more current information. The selling agent was hard to contact, and just after we had viewed the pub and said we were really interested the vendors went off on holiday, leaving everything up in the air. It was clear that the vendors were not willing to explain matters, and the agent was not interested in expending any effort in our direction. Someone else was interested, and whether or not they had spotted this problem we don't know, but we let this one drop at the end of January. You can't buy anything if the seller isn't interested in selling!!

Pubs Four and Five bite the dust – but Pub One returns...

Around Christmas we found Pub Four – a leasehold pub in a tourist village and again an absolutely ideal building and surroundings. This we visited, viewed and examined the accounts, thought about it, and our consultants did an Outlet Assessment. (Yes, to your surprise we are still using the same consultant....) We talked it over in-depth, did all the right things, and then and put in an offer which was agreed in principle. The accounts were the exact opposite of those of Pub Three – immaculate and right up-to-date, they had clearly been prepared by someone who had, from Day One, been determined to present the business in the best possible light when it came to sell. The husband and wife team who have built up this pub so well have found another challenge just up the valley in the shape of a premises they have long wanted to own coming available and want to move on.

We are on our way, Pub Four it is to be!!

Then the vendors went off on holiday (how can people go on holiday in the middle of selling their business?), and we had to wait over two weeks before they could progress matters.

In the meantime, you might have thought that Pub One had gone away, but no! On 17 February Viv spoke to our licensing solicitor who had handled our licence application for Pub One, to ask him if he could/would act if we are successful with Pub Four, which was in his area. By pure coincidence he had been in the magistrates' court the previous day on an entirely unconnected matter and to his amazement someone had stood up and applied for and got a Protection Order transferring the Pub One licence away from Viv to his client – who is our consultant!!

To do this would (normally) have needed Viv's written agreement (as Viv had got the written permission of the previous landlord when she applied for the transfer of licence in October) – but she had not given this permission, nor even been asked for it. The person in court had, we are told, stood up and said that permission had been sought and willingly given when the idea had never even mentioned by the applicants. A lie in court, no less, which the magistrates accepted without question.

Later, our solicitor called to say he had also been in court when the owners of Pub One (that is Brewery 1) had phoned to apologise for not having put in an application to renew the licence in its name – the consultant is buying the pub and appears to have forged Viv's agreement to the licence transfer, while the owners think the licence is in their name!! And we hear the police are going to object to renewal anyway....

(This was the time – it happens every three years – when all pub licences have to be renewed in front of the magistrates. Our (private) strategy was now, as we could not buy the pub as we had been so badly deceived, to simply not apply for the renewal of Viv's licence. It would thus automatically lapse and the pub would cease to be a pub and could not be re-licensed because of the car park planning conditions. Brewery 1 thought the licence was in its name (which it never had been) and apologised to the court for not giving notice of its intention to renew by the due date and asked for a concession; the consultant, knowing this "renewal" date was imminent was trying to get the licence off Viv before it lapsed - complicated??!!)

So we wrote to the consultants saying "no way and foul", and asked our solicitor to once again act on our behalf to object to this transfer. As far as everyone else is concerned, we are not letting go of the licence, unless we have to, without considerable compensation for the trouble deliberately, we believe, caused.

Ironically, the consultant had come back into the picture a few days earlier. Mindful that they had not done much relative to their contract with us on Pub One and that we were obliged to pay the second half of the agreed fee when we finally get a pub. Viv and I had twice visited its offices separately to see what was happening and got not very far, but its newly-appointed head "pub finding man" (from now on is referred to as consultancy man) had been off sick. As soon as he returned we asked him to come and see us and voiced our concerns at past service. He sprang into action and undertook a viability study on both Pubs Three and Four (we were interested in both at the time) promising them for 11 February. Then we discarded Pub Three, and the consultant's MD was said to be "tweaking the study for Pub Four", but as of today, 19 February, there is no sign of it, and, of course, given the above tale regarding the licence will we hear from them in a civil tone again?

(In the main text of the book I warn against consultants who have both pub-finding and pub-operating or renovating activities, as there is surely a conflict of interest. In the time since we set about assessing the refurbishment work needed on Pub One, the consultants had started a pub renovating/operating arm in partnership with one of the builders who had come to look at Pub One with a view to working on it, and it was to this partnership that the licence was being transferred.)

Through our solicitor we sought considerable compensation for Viv to agree to the transfer of the licence, a sum which consultancy man agreed was a fair way ahead given the circumstances. The consultants had agreed a purchase price well below what we had bid, were not being held to a tie by Brewery 1, and, even more amazingly, had done a finance deal with Brewery 2 which we had been prevented from doing. The sum we asked for would have effectively repaid our expenses in getting this far on Pub One, while still giving the consultant a far better deal, as well as our continuing good will and custom, that would otherwise have been the case.

So, as of 19 February 1998 we have an offer in on Pub Four and no other in the possibles pile. Next week will be crucial, and doubtless Pub One will rumble on, too.

...and on to Pub Five

The next diary entry is dated 11 March 1998.

You might not have thought this could get any more complex.

Well, the owners of Pub Four came back off holiday, and duly found out, a bit late in the day if you ask me, that they could not afford the pub they said they were going to, given the figures in its latest accounts. So that has gone into total limbo and we have not heard from them since.

(Readers will recall that our pub-buying saga started some months ago because, in essence, our existing business was doing badly: it has got no better, we are spending a great deal of time researching pubs, so we need an income from somewhere even more urgently.)

Realising that we were still no nearer our goal, we again contacted all the relevant estate agents and asked for any new pub sales details.

The response included the monthly newspaper from one of the major agents in which was a pub headlined "Cheshire commuter village". We had not had the details before as it was not in our chosen geographic area, but this now became our Pub Five. It was certainly well worth a look.

So, the newspaper arrived on Monday 2 March, the details were faxed over that morning and we went off to see it that lunchtime. It is absolutely ideal, with brilliant trading areas and a very affluent clientele. The only obvious drawback is the smallish domestic accommodation. At 1pm on that wet Monday lunchtime there were over 40 people in the pub, many of them eating. We did a formal viewing the following day and indicated we were very interested. We went back on the Friday lunch for another look, and we counted well over 70 customers.

Then, as always, there was a snag – the accounts were awful! The landlord told us the pub had been closed for a year or more and that he had refurbished it, got rid of the drugs element and turned it into an up-market pub for the extremely prosperous local residents and office workers. It had, he said, been trading for exactly three years in this guise, and he was only selling because his wife had hurt her back and could not pull her weight in the business as well as looking after their two young children. He seemed very upset at the prospect of having to leave. When we met his wife she lifted and carried the two-year-old without any seeming discomfort.

According to the accounts a turnover of £300,000 was achieved in the first year after re-opening (from a cold start), and this fell slightly in years two and three – hardly a likely scenario. But the rent rose dramatically last year and there is almost no profit, hence the low asking price. Our accountant feels these accounts shown are not genuine: the trade is certainly there from personal observation, but it does seem "summat's up".

As I write, the closing date for offers (the landlord wants out in a hurry and we are given to believe – as is usual – there are others interested) is next Monday. We shall put in an offer, but whether it is sensible to do so given the accounts is another matter. Everyone we can think of is asking questions for us to try and find out "the whys and wherefores" behind the veil, so to speak.

Onward to 24 March 1998

On Friday 13 March we visited Pub Five with consultancy man, monitored activity over lunch and then he had a good talk with the landlord. The result was that he agreed to accept our offer – at £72,000 it is just below the asking price of £75,000, but we agreed an additional £5000 cash-in-hand. The formal part of the offer was duly presented to the agent on Monday lunchtime, just before the deadline, and duly accepted the following day – the most professional bid the agents had seen in a long time, they said!!

So now we proceed as fast as we can. Of course there are hiccups – consultancy man was going to come round on 20 March with the assessment study, but it was eventually faxed over on Tuesday morning (today). We hear the brewery landlords want an £8000 bond paid as an added item on the rent, rather than up front as we had heard they would – we have the bond already locked away in a Building Society, but this means 25% on the rent on top of the 66% rise which was imposed less than a year ago. This is Pub One all over again!!

Different values

We met with Graham and Abi Tillotson on Sunday evening on our way back from seeing my dad. Graham and I were at Primary and Sunday schools together, and having not seen each other since college days re-met about three years ago.

We have had broadly similar lives – he has degree-level education and has had a career in engineering, although civil rather than aerospace. His father was the local bank manager when I was at school, so like me he had a very upright upbringing. And like Viv and I are planning to do, Graham and Abi have changed tack recently, as noted at the beginning of this diary.

So on Sunday evening we got talking about how I was having difficulty with the basic ways of the pub industry, which is essentially to assume from the outset that everyone is a cheat, a liar and a scoundrel, until you are sure otherwise, and in the meantime take them for what you can. In engineering it is broadly the opposite – you assume what you are told is true, take the person's word and, in many cases, trust your life on this intrinsic assumption.

As Abi said, you have to get used to different values. In their city centre chip shop they come across many people who are chauvinistic in the extreme – husbands who won't let their wives eat fish, only the chips, and who regularly beat them up as a matter of almost daily routine. And, of course, "only men fry fish" – Abi does all the frying at "Dennis's Fish & Chip Shop" near Leeds market (highly recommended), which is very unusual and causes raised eyebrows. Different values, and ones we four, because of our upbringing and social class, do not relate to. But if you go into another industry, outside your roots, you have to accept their ways, you cannot change them. By being a professional person frying fish in a city centre chippy you are not going to change years of male-dominant assumptions, and nor are we going to change the assumptions of lying and deceit we find to be endemic in the pub trade. If we want to run a pub, we have to go with the flow, take the hits and learn how to screw them back – after all, we have the brains on our side!!

Good advice indeed, and as Abi says we have to take the plunge, take the knocks and go with it, or not at all!!

★★

The (unexpected) end

That week, the one ending Friday 27 March saw the sudden end of our pub plans....

After we met Graham and Abi, Viv and I had two funerals on successive days – Viv's aunt Win in Luton on Wednesday, and my aunt Joan in Halifax on Thursday. That set us in a serious and thinking mood.

On the Wednesday we received a shock letter from consultancy man. On our way to Pub Five with him on 13 March he made several mobile phone calls while driving, and had had little time to talk. He had been strangely silent while assessing the pub.

He had said he would return to our house with us straight after the visit to discuss things, but instead met with contacts en route and left us to catch the bus – this was OK as he said he would be coming onto our house after that meeting. But instead he phoned saying he would see us the following Friday, the 20th, with the draft business plan. Surprise, surprise, this wasn't ready on time, so that meeting was cancelled and rearranged for the 27th – a two week delay for a conversation we should have had in the pub car park.

On the Tuesday, the 24th, he faxed through the business plan, which was pretty good, certainly far better than they had done for Pub One. But then came a faxed letter saying that he was charging us £5000 extra to cover past services, and he wanted "a substantial amount" when he visited on Friday. He knew full well we were off to funerals and this £5000 was seemingly linked to our demand for money to agree to the transfer of the Pub One licence. (The total consultancy fee, as stipulated in the contract, was just over £1500, of which half had been paid at the very start: in all honesty the consultancy had put in a very large number of hours for the £750 so far paid, but then if they had been more pro-active on Pub One we would have been in and trading a long time ago and they would be enjoying our continuing patronage.)

So we told him not to come, that there was no extra money, and that we didn't want to see him again, full stop. Which left us alone working on Pub Five. (One thing we had agreed with the consultancy, which we would recommend to readers, was that the "training man", who had considerable experience managing pubs, would come and live with us for our first three weeks at Pub Five, while we learned the ropes. We certainly could not contemplate starting business without such help, and this person would have been ideal.)

We could get no response from the brewery-owners to our request for a meeting – the brewery requires to vet prospective tenants before any deal can go through, and the legal side of Pub Five was racing ahead without any feedback at all from the brewery. We were within perhaps a week of exchanging contracts without any hint as to whether the brewery would accept us, or as to what their training or vetting requirements would be.

On the Friday afternoon we visited our bank, where a new manager, Tony, had replaced Doug who had taken early retirement. Tony was very good and supportive, but he is a totally different character; he is much more cautious than his predecessor, and, when, towards the end he said the interest rate on the loan we needed would be quite a bit higher than previously agreed, and interest rates are rising anyway, we took that as a "double caution".

Over the weekend we discussed the situation and decided the bastards had won. Clearly we need a consultant to help us get underway, and we cannot trust the one we had stuck with throughout. The rises in (effective) rent and bank loan interest rate on Pub Five meant that no-one was on our side, and we decided without anyone at all rooting for us, we would get nowhere.

So on Sunday 29 March we threw it all away.

So far, and today is 15 April 1998, there has been no come-back apart from a hefty – but fair!! – bill from our solicitors who were working very quickly on Pub Five. I am sure there will be more to this tale.

Meanwhile, on 8 April, the consultants finally got the licence of Pub One despite our strong objections. Our solicitor made the magistrates aware that the place is in breach of the planning conditions, but that did not cut ice with them, and they believed the MD's undertakings that that problem would be sorted out.

As of today, 15 April, we are very happy we made the decision to "stop pubs". We are trying to get back publishing work but we are still going to sell this house, some time, and move on. With all we have found out about the trade, pubs simply are not for us. *(But they may well be for you, you must evaluate your own experiences as you follow the trail.)* It has been a very expensive nine months, but some good lessons have been learnt and we've gained a lot of experience. Should we have done it? – undoubtedly yes, at this point, for we tried to take on a new life, found it wasn't going to work and pulled out without harm, except that of having an even lower bank balance. *(And in January 1999, another nine months on, those words are still true as far as we are concerned.)*

I am sure I shall be writing more, even though this saga is effectively over.

The final irony?

As I complete these words it is now September 1998 and to my great surprise there have been no further developments. I have, so far, been unable to get any answer from the council as to why or if Pub One is to be allowed to trade when it breaches its planning agreement, but that is now all rather irrelevant. *(The council did later write to say permission had been refused and a revised application was being considered.)*

But there has been one final twist in the saga, which only serves to illustrate the way the licensed trade operates.

Going back only to Pub Five, you will recall that the asking price was £75,000, and that we agreed with the owner a sum of £72,000, plus £5000 in cash "in his back pocket" for his kind consideration of our offer. We were told more than once, and in the usual firm tones, that if our bid fell down there were plenty of other interested parties. All these had, of course, more, and more readily available, money, and were eagerly waiting in the wings to take our place.

Thus, while we greatly dislike letting people down we did not feel too bad when were obliged to give back-word, as there were all these others who would rapidly bale out the landlord from whatever problems he might have had.

Having read our saga, you might not be too surprised to hear that, some three months after we pulled out, the selling estate agent once again sent us the details for this pub. Still on the market, and at the reduced price of £68,000....

A very good way to bring an end to the diary!!

The doors are locked

The majority of the words for this book were committed to the word processor in June 1998 while Viv was away working. It then lay in abeyance for some time while it was checked over by our solicitors and accountant. In the meantime, we learned that aunt Joan, mentioned above, had so very kindly left us a small legacy in her Will, and this has enabled us to use our publishing skills to take this project forward. As a result, the final tidying up of the text is being done over the Christmas week, 1998. As far as we know Pub One is still not trading, the local council having blocked re-opening, or so we are told, because of the car park planning conditions, which they are refusing to change. The consultants discovered almost immediately after we withdrew our interest that the old railway carriage which was attached to the building as a restaurant contained blue asbestos, something which had not been brought to our attention and which our surveyor had missed. As far as I am aware it is illegal to sell anything which contains blue asbestos, which has to be removed by highly-specialised contractors. When I last visited the site a couple of months ago, the carriage, worth perhaps £30,000 in the railway preservation movement, had been taken away for scrap, while the pub was still boarded up, some 15 months after we first saw it.

We sold my parents' former house earlier this year, but have had no luck selling our house in Bury, so had we bought a pub we would have had huge borrowings for a very long time, with horrendous consequences. And ironically our publishing business has gained new life, and we are working all over Christmas to keep pace.

Just as we would have been doing had we been landlords....

Driving Home

A SHAGGY DOG STORY

Well, I hope you have enjoyed your visit to the theatre that has been the stage for this humble book. I am sure there is a very good, and highly sociable living to be made running a pub, but there are lessons to learn all along the way. The life wasn't for us, it may well be for you and I wish you every success and happiness if you choose to go this way.

But having visited the theatre and taken on board the moral of the tale, imagine, dear reader, you are now driving home and mulling over all you have seen and heard. Perhaps a joke will keep your spirits up (or even your orange-and-lemonades if you are teetotal) and help take your mind off the stony road ahead.

It is not a new joke, it is in fact one of the oldest jokes I can recall being told, and that goes back a few years! It is a shaggy dog story, and as we have just bought a shaggy dog and it involves a publican, it seems an appropriate way to fill the last two pages.

In a beautiful pub in an even more beautiful Yorkshire Dales village, for where else could a shaggy dog story be set, lived a landlord, a landlady and their happy family. Very much a part of the family was Mac, a shaggy dog of some renown, for Mac was said by all to be the most handsome dog in the whole of the Dale.

Mac was loved by all who came into the pub, for this was a part of the world not frequented by those from the Nanny State, the Protect People from Themselves Society, or even the HSE, and dogs were properly allowed in this pub, and children were properly not. No-one loved Mac more than his owner, John the jovial landlord, but everyone who came into the pub, local or tourist, gave Mac a friendly pat and remarked how handsome he was. Mac's fame spread the length of the Dale, yes, even as far as Ripon.

Mac spent many a happy year in the bar, wagging his tale at unsuspecting (and suspecting) customers and scrounging the odd crisp or three. He was even known to lap up a bowl of Black Sheep or Timothy Taylor's Landlord every so often, only the best for our Mac!! But sadly the day dawned which was to be Mac's last in this world, and at a grand old age he slipped peacefully towards Doggie Heaven.

John, and indeed the whole family, nay the whole village, was distraught, and wondered what to do so that Mac could be best remembered. After a Village Meeting it was decided to bury Mac in the churchyard with full honours, but first John was to be allowed to cut off Mac's magnificent tail, or was it tale, his most memorable feature, and place it in a fine oak and brass case "the best you have, Mr Undertaker, t' one wi' brass handles", to be mounted above the bar for all to admire.

The deed was done, and, unknown of course to all, Mac made his way slowly to Doggie Heaven. At The Pearly Gates, or maybe they are Bonio Gates, (named after Bill of that ilk, not known for his love of Macs, gettit??) he was greeted by St. Peter Dog, who had all his records in front of him and was very impressed, as you would expect.

"Well, Mac," said St. Peter, "You have been a good dog - fifteen years' loyal service to your master, loved by everyone and not a single entry in your Human Bite Record Book. Well done indeed!! Of course you are most welcome in Doggie Heaven..... err, but wait a moment."

Mac paused, or was it pawsed, as he passed into the world beyond, for St. Peter had noticed something - Mac had no tail!!

"Er, wo, Mac, but we seem to have a problem here, said Houston, St Peter's Main Man. "You are indeed the most splendid dog, but God Dog is very much of the Old School (Roundhay Grammar, the best, then) and doesn't allow partly-dressed dogs in, and you are singularly lacking in the tail department. I'm sorry, you can't come in, rules is rules, it's the Other World for you, the one where all the PC dogs go. Sorry." (PC dogs – those that aren't Macs, *Ed*)

Mac was aghast. "Oh please'" he woofed, "I have been ever such a good dog, can't the rules be bent, just for me. I have been trying so hard to be good enough for Doggie Heaven – perhaps my tail will grow again...."

"No, sorry, more than my job's worth."

"Oh, go on, just one more chance. Perhaps if I went back to my master he would give me my tail back??"

And so it was. God Dog was consulted, a meeting of the Celestial Kennel was convened and a Grand Vote taken. Mac, in recognition of his outstanding services, was to be allowed one half-hour visit back to his former home.

It was just after two in the morning when John was awoken from a deep sleep (as if landlords get deep sleeps, you can tell this is a joke!!) by what sounded like a whining and scratching at the front door. And the more John listened, the more he thought to himself, "I know that whine, can it be...."

It was. John went downstairs, opened the door and there was his now tail-less partner of 15 years. "Mac!" he exclaimed, "can it really be thissen, how wonderful to see thee, but how can it be, it isn't yet twelve hours since we buried thee in t'graveyard – look, tha tail is above bar, for all to see!"

"Well, oh master, that is what I have come to see you about". Mac told the tale of St Peter Dog and what had happened at The

Bonio Gates, and "...and so if I could have my tail back, I shall be allowed in Doggie Heaven, where I've always wanted to be."

A tear came to John's eyes, indeed they flooded down his cheeks. "I am sorry, Mac, you have been a wonderful dog, no man could ask for better, and nothing would give me more pleasure than to oblige. But you know how keen that new young policeman in the village is, and you know the law.

No re-tailing spirits after hours."